R Programming for Beginners

An Introduction to Learn R Programming with Tutorials and Hands-On Examples

Text Copyright © Light Bulb Publishing

All rights reserved. No part of this guide may be reproduced in any form without permission in writing from the publisher except in the case of brief quotations embodied in critical articles or reviews.

Legal & Disclaimer

The information contained in this book and its contents is not designed to replace or take the place of any form of medical or professional advice; and is not meant to replace the need for independent medical, financial, legal or other professional advice or services, as may be required. The content and information in this book has been provided for educational and entertainment purposes only.

The content and information contained in this book has been compiled from sources deemed reliable, and it is accurate to the best of the Author's knowledge, information, and belief. However, the Author cannot guarantee its accuracy and validity and cannot be held liable for any errors and/or omissions. Further, changes are periodically made to this book as and when needed. Where appropriate and/or necessary, you must consult a professional (including but not limited to your doctor, attorney, financial advisor or such other professional advisor) before using any of the suggested remedies, techniques, or information in this book.

Upon using the contents and information contained in this book, you agree to hold harmless the Author from and against any damages, costs, and expenses, including any legal fees potentially resulting from the application of any of the information provided by this book. This disclaimer applies to any loss, damages or injury caused by the use and application, whether directly or indirectly, of any advice or information presented, whether for breach of contract, tort, negligence, personal injury, criminal intent, or under any other cause of action.

You agree to accept all risks of using the information presented in this book.

You agree that by continuing to read this book, where appropriate and/or necessary, you shall consult a professional (including but not limited to your doctor, attorney, or financial advisor or such other advisor as needed) before using any of the suggested remedies, techniques, or information in this book.

Table of Contents

1. Introduction 1
2. Scope of R 3
3. Getting Started 5
   3.1 Install R Environment 5
   3.2 Executing R Scripts 12
4. Syntax 15
   4.1 Statements 15
   4.2 Blocks 15
   4.3 Comments 16
   4.4 Keywords 17
5. Hello World! R Script 19
6. Data Types 21
7. Variables 23
   7.1 Variable Assignment 24
   7.2 Displaying Variables 25
   7.3 Data Type of a Variable 27
8. Operators 29
   8.1 Arithmetic Operators 30
   8.2 Relational Operators 32
   8.3 Logical Operators 33
   8.4 Assignment Operators 35
9. R Terminal 37
10. User Input 39

11. Vectors and Lists 43
11.1 Vectors 43
11.2 Lists 49
12. Control Structures 53
12.1 Decision making 53
12.2 Loops 60
13. Functions 67
13.1 Function Definition 67
13.2 Function Call 69
13.3 Default Arguments 73
13.4 Nested Function Calls 74
13.5 Using switch() function effectively 74
14. Strings 77
14.1 String Formation 77
14.2 String Concatenation 77
14.3 Substring 78
14.4 Miscellaneous String Operations 79
15. Factors 81
16. Data Frames 83
16.1 Accessing Data from Data Frames 87
16.2 Factors in Data Frames 90
16.3 Structure and Summary 93
16.4 Data Frame Modification 94
16.5 Conditional Access of Data Frame Records 100
16.6 Access Data Frames with Loops 102

17. Basic File Handling 105
17.1 Current Working Directory 105
17.2 Working with files and directories 107
18. Data Interfaces 111
18.1 CSV Data Interface 111
18.2 Excel Data Interface 125
19. Data Visualization 133
19.1 Pie Chart 133
19.2 Bar Chart 140
19.3 Line Graph 144
20. Programming Examples 149
20.1 Sum, Average and Greatest element of a vector. 149
20.2 Factorial 150
20.3 Reverse a given number 151
20.4 CSV to XLSX File conversion 152
20.5 Sine Wave Generation 153
21. Final Words 157

1. Introduction

R is an object oriented scripting language that provides an environment for statistical computing. While *R* can also be used as a general purpose programming language, the features that it provides are well suited and are very useful for statistical computing.

In 1976, a programming language called *S* was developed by *John Chambers* at *Bell Laboratories*. *R* is an implementation of *S* programming language developed by *Ross Ihaka* and *Robert Gentleman* at the *University of Auckland, New Zealand*. At present, *R* is developed and maintained by *R Development Core Team*. *R* being an implementation of *S* programming language, most of *S* code should run in *R* environment.

R is completely open source and is released with a *GNU General Public License*. As an end user, you do not have to build R using its source code as pre-compiled binaries are available for Windows, Linux and MAC.

When learning R, some previous programming experience will definitely help but is not mandatory. However, you should be comfortable with using your system, be it Windows, Linux or MAC; especially be comfortable with using the *Command Prompt* on Windows and *Terminal/Shell* on MAC/Linux. Apart from general purpose programming, this book also covers statistical computing. Hence, some knowledge of statistics is needed to understand relevant sections.

2. Scope of R

R is mostly used for statistical computing, data analytics, data visualization and in relevant fields but in general, R can more or less do all the basic things that any other scripting language such as Python, Perl, Ruby, etc. can do. By basic I mean perform logical/arithmetic operations, interact with the user, access files on the system, etc. Having said that, R cannot do things like lower level system operations such as memory manipulation; there is no native framework to build a GUI or work with web projects. Despite these drawbacks what makes R special is that it can easily be extended using packages. It is also possible to interact with R code using other programming languages such as C/C++, Java, Python, etc. This feature opens up a whole new possibility of using R almost everywhere. For example, consider a user has some data and wants to plot a histogram. You can write code in R to accept data and plot the histogram in the backend and build a GUI front end using any framework of your choice (that is supported by R) such as VB.NET/C# .NET, Qt C++, etc. The user will provide data through the GUI (which is not built using R), the GUI will send the data to the R script where the histogram will be plotted and sent back to the GUI for the user to see. Alternatively, you can build a nice website using HTML/CSS/JS which will let a user to upload data, receive this data using Python CGI script, call the R code via Python, get the histogram, sent it back to the webpage. The possibilities of R integration with other languages/frameworks is endless! You can look at R as a feature rich computing environment.

Databases such as MySQL, Oracle, PostgreSQL, etc. can be accessed using R with the help of the relevant drivers. With this feature and powerful data analytics, data visualization and statistical tools, R is a very powerful programming language for Data Science and Big Data.

In this book, you will learn about basics of R and some basics of statistical computing using R. Integration of R with other languages and databases is not covered as it would also need good knowledge of other programming languages and databases in question.

3. Getting Started

R is an interpreted language and hence R interpreter is needed for programs to work. The interpreter is available via a command line interface but there also exists several integrated development environments (IDEs) such as **RStudio** which provides many more tools that can be used for purposes other than just writing and executing scripts. We will only use the R interpreter for executing our programs. A R program/script can be written using any text editor such as **Notepad**. I recommend using **Notepad++** (https://notepad-plus-plus.org/). Simple R programs/script files have the extensions of **.r** or **.R**. There are other extensions such as **.RData, .rds and .rda** about which we will learn in the appropriate sections.

3.1 Install R Environment

The R environment is available for Windows, Linux and MAC. We will be using a Windows PC to write and execute R programs. R script written on one OS shall work seamlessly on other OS as long as there is no OS specific code. In order to install R environment, download the latest installation file from https://www.r-project.org/ under the Download section. At the time of writing this book (July 2019), the latest R release is **3.6.1** and the downloads are hosted by CRAN mirror servers. Once you have the installation file, log into your system with an account that has administrative privileges, execute the file, select language if asked and you will be presented with the following window:

Click *Next* and you will see a window which will let you set the installation location of R:

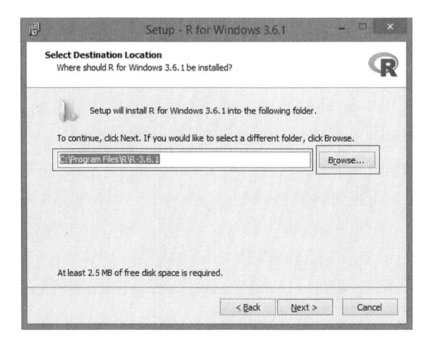

3. Getting Started

If you must install R at a custom location, then either enter the exact path or click *Browse* and pick the destination directory of your choice. It is best to leave the destination unchanged. Click *Next* to proceed.

Do not change anything in the next few steps unless you know what you are doing, simply keep clicking *Next*.

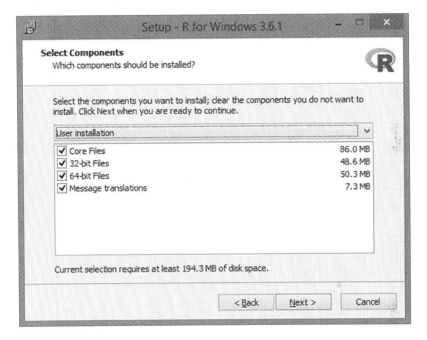

R Programming for Beginners

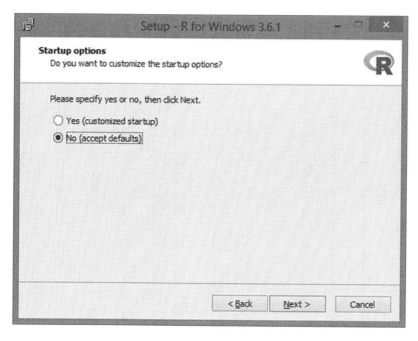

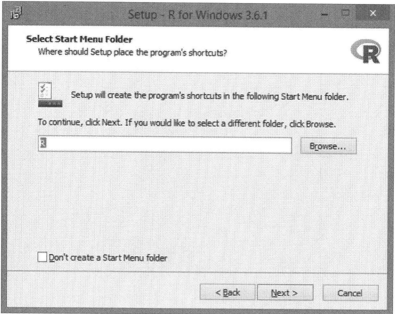

3. Getting Started

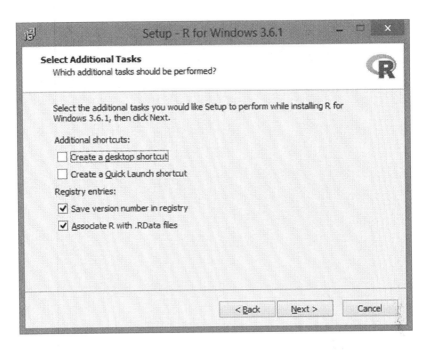

When you click *Next* in this step, the installation process will begin and may take a few minutes.

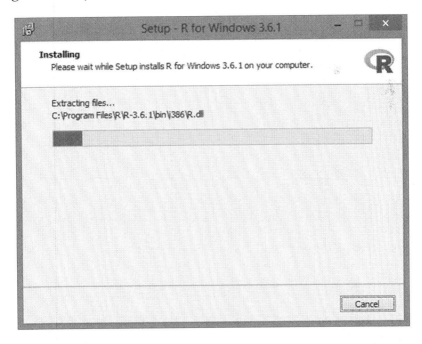

Once the installation process has finished, it is time to set environment variables.

Open *System Properties* (*Windows Key + Pause Break*) and click on *Advanced system settings*. You will see a window like this:

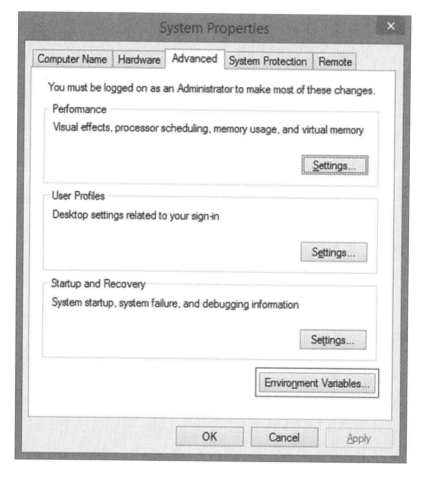

Click *Environment Variables*. You will see a window like this:

3. Getting Started

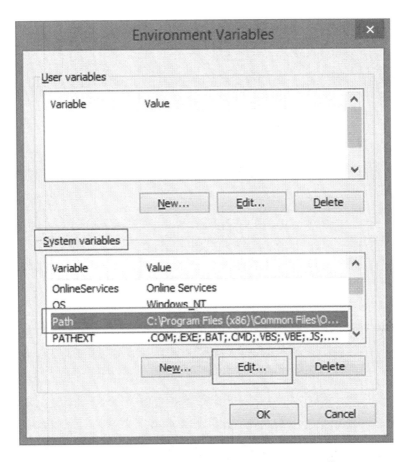

Under *System variable*, click *Path* and click *Edit*. A window will open which will let you manipulate the *Path* environment variable.

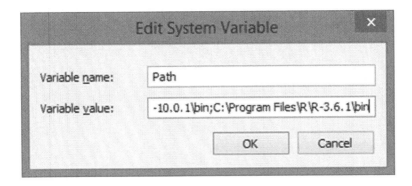

In the *Variable value* field, append R's bin directory *<R installation Directory>\R-3.6.1\bin* at the end after the semicolon. If you left destination directory unchanged during installation, the bin directory will be *C:\Program Files\R\R-3.6.1\bin*. Click *OK* and close all other system windows by clicking *OK*.

Open *Command Prompt*, type *R* and hit *Enter*. If you see an error message like – *"R" is not recognized as an internal or external command, operable program or batch file*, it means either R has not been properly installed or the *Path* variable has not been properly set. In such a case, go through this section again.

If you see something like this:

```
F:\>R
R version 3.6.1 (2019-07-05) -- "Action of the Toes"
Copyright (C) 2019 The R Foundation for Statistical Computing
Platform: x86_64-w64-mingw32/x64 (64-bit)

R is free software and comes with ABSOLUTELY NO WARRANTY.
You are welcome to redistribute it under certain conditions.
Type 'license()' or 'licence()' for distribution details.

  Natural language support but running in an English locale

R is a collaborative project with many contributors.
Type 'contributors()' for more information and
'citation()' on how to cite R or R packages in publications.

Type 'demo()' for some demos, 'help()' for on-line help, or
'help.start()' for an HTML browser interface to help.
Type 'q()' to quit R.

>
```

It means R has been successfully installed, the Path variable has been correctly set and you have successfully started the R Terminal.

3.2 Executing R Scripts

A R script/program can be written using any text editor and should be saved as file with the extension *.r* or *.R*. This file is called as R script/program, source code, program or source. This is an idle source file and will not execute on its own. In order to execute this file, you need to make use of the ***Rscript*** command. ***Rscript*** is command-line utility for executing R scripts supplied with R installation on Windows, Linux and MAC. On Windows, it is available as ***Rscript.exe*** and is present in *<R installation Directory>\R-3.6.1\bin*; on Linux and MAC, ***Rscript*** is available as an executable binary. This is how R scripts are executed using ***Rscript*** command via ***Command Prompt*** on Windows and ***Shell/Terminal*** on Linux/MAC:

Rscript <path to .r file>
Eg:
Rscript demo.r

Let us understand the process of R script execution with an example. Open your favourite text editor, copy-paste the following code:

```
#This is my first program
print ("This is my first program!")
```

This code prints a message; you do not have to understand the working of this script at present. You will learn each of these concepts in detail as you go through the chapters. For now, you just have to understand how R scripts are executed. Save the file as ***firstprogram.r***. This is our R script and we will execute it using ***Rscript*** command. Open ***Command Prompt*** on Windows or ***Shell/Terminal*** on Linux/MAC and navigate to the directory where ***firstprogram.r*** has been saved using ***cd*** command. Enter the following command:

Rscript firstprogram.r

With this command, the program should execute and you should see something like this:

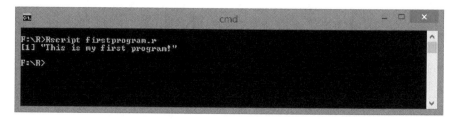

You can give the entire path to R script if you have not navigated to the directory where R script is placed as shown below:

Rscript F:\R\firstprogram.r

The result will be the same:

The process of executing an R script across Windows, Linux and MAC remains the same and is quite straight forward. Following up to this step is crucial because you will be executing several R scripts throughout the course of this book.

4. Syntax

R is a case-sensitive scripting language. We may look at these words – "eBook" and "ebook" and say that they are the same but to an R interpreter, these two words are different and are treated differently.

4.1 Statements

A statement in a programming language is used to carry out a certain task. A task could be anything such as adding two numbers, displaying a message on the screen, performing statistical operation, etc. In R, one statement is written on one line. You can have multiple statements on a line by separating them using semi-colons but it is best to avoid this method. Here are a few examples of statements in R:

```
var <- 125
print ("This is a sample statement.")
a <- 5.8
b <- 8.67
c <- a * b
```

4.2 Blocks

A block is a collection of several lines of code enclosed within curly brackets ({ }). Here is an example of a code block:

```
{
    A <- A + 1
    print ("This is a code block!")
}
```

Blocks are used extensively while working with decision making, loops, functions, etc.

4.3 Comments

Comments are used to mark/describe a piece of code and are ignored by the interpreter. This means, comments are inconsequential when it comes to the execution of a script. R offers single line comments as well as multi-line comments.

4.3.1 Single Line Comments

A single line comment begins with a *hash symbol (#)* and terminates on the same line. Here is an example:

#This is a single line comment.

4.3.2 Multi-Line Comments

Multi-line comments span over several lines and are enclosed within single or double quotes. Here is an example:

"This is a multi-line comment.
Next line begins here.
Another line in this multi-line comment."
    OR
'This is another way of writing a multi-line comment
Should end with a single quote'

Note: All the programs included in this book make extensive use of comments to explain what a particular piece of code does. Make sure you read them carefully in order to understand the programs in the best possible way.

4.4 Keywords

Keywords are reserved words which cannot be used to name variables, functions, etc. Here is a list of all the available keywords in R:

if	else	repeat	while	function
for	in	next	break	TRUE
FALSE	NULL	Inf	NaN	NA
NA_integer_	NA_real_	NA_complex_	NA_character_	...

5. Hello World! R Script

The execution of an R script happens in a top-down manner. That is, the execution will begin from the first statement and all the following statements will be executed one by one until the last one. If you have come from a programming background having written programs in C, C++, Java, etc. you will know that there has to be a *main* function that serves as an entry point of the program. There is no such thing in R.

In this section we will learn to write our first R script – a script to display *Hello World!* There is a function called *print* which is used to display data on the screen. We will learn about different ways of using this function throughout the course of this book as and when required. For now, let us see how can we use the *print* function to display *Hello World!* text on the screen.

The syntax of print function for this case:

print (<text>)

Hello World! is a text. In programmatic terms, text is a string (sequence of characters). In R, string constants are represented by enclosing text within double quotes. The text *Hello World!* can be represented as *"Hello World!"* as a constant string. In order to display Hello World! using print function, the following statement can be used:

print ("Hello World!")

Let us put this in a program, save it as *HelloWorld.r* and execute it. Here is how the program should look like:

```
#This is a Hello World R script
#This script displays the message Hello World! on the screen
print ("Hello World!")
```

Open command-prompt/terminal/shell, navigate to the directory where you have saved this program and execute this script using the ***Rscript*** command as follows:

Rscript HelloWorld.r

Output:

Having read till this chapter, you should now be able to write, save and execute R programs. If you still have problems with any of the concepts discussed till now, it is advisable to go through all the chapters again. We have also seen how to use the ***print*** function to display text on the screen. I suggest you write a few more scripts and execute them, use the print function to display different messages and learn to use comments.

6. Data Types

A data type defines the kind of data we are working with. For example, if we want to store the name and age of a person, name will be a string and age will be a number. These two are different data types. Similarly, there are various data types for different types of data. R supports 6 basic data types and many derived data types. Derived data types are formed using basic data types and some of them are also called as data structures. In this section, we will learn briefly about the 6 basic data types. These will be better understood in the next chapter. Covering each and every derived data type is not possible and hence the important ones are covered as and when required through the course of this book.

Here is a table that describes the 6 basic data types:

Data Type	Description	Example
Numeric	Numeric values, real or floating point types.	4, 86.654, 0.003, 4532
Integer	Used for storing integers only.	0L, 777L, 243L
Complex	Complex numbers, must carry real and imaginary parts.	2+3i, -5+6i, 4-22i, -15-7i
Character	Used for strings. Values must be enclosed in single or double quotes. Character and string is used interchangeably in this book.	"x", "Hello", 'eBook', "iPhone", 'LG'
Logical	Boolean values of TRUE or FALSE.	TRUE, FALSE
Raw	Used to store values in hexadecimal form.	The word "Awesome" will be stored as 41 77 65 73 6f 6d 65

7. Variables

A variable is a name given to a memory location. When a variable is declared, based on its data type, some memory is reserved for it in the system. Most of the times, memory locations are addressed using hexadecimal addresses and they are quite lengthy. The concept of variables makes sure that we do not have to remember the addresses of the memory locations. In other words, you can say that a variable name is an alias of a memory location.

In R, you do not have to specify the data type of a variable as it is extracted implicitly based on the type of the data stored inside a variable. You do not even have to declare a variable, simply assigning a value to a variable will be considered as declaration and assignment or initialization in other words.

Rules of naming a variable:

- A variable name can contain letters (upper and lower case) and numbers.

- The only special characters allowed in a variable name are dot (.) and underscore (_).

- A variable name cannot start with a number or an underscore.

- A variable name can start with a dot but cannot be followed by a number.

- Reserved words (*Section 4.4*) cannot be used as variable names.

Here are a few examples of valid variable names – age, country, first_name, last_name, data1, data.2, .var.2, totalScore, Miles.

Note: Everything in R is an object.

7.1 Variable Assignment

There are three ways of assigning values to variables using the following operators – **equal to operator (=), leftwards operator (<-), rightwards operator (->)**. When using equal to and leftward operator, the variable is present on the left hand side and the value is present on the right hand side, the assignment works in a right-to-left manner. When using the rightward operator, the value to be assigned in on the left hand side and the variable is present on the right hand side, the assignment works in a left-to-right manner.

Here is the syntax of using these operators:

#Equal-to Operator
[variable] = [value/expression/variable]
Example:
Name = "Bonnie"
age = 25
weight = 54.75

#Leftwards Operator
[variable] <- [value/expression/variable]
Example:
Country <- "Canada"
Zip_Code <- "V5K0A3"

7. Variables

#Rightwards Operator

[value/expression/variable] -> [variable]

Example:

"Vancouver" -> City

172.5 -> height

7.2 Displaying Variables

The *print* function which we studied in **Section 5** is good enough to display one variable at a time. Syntax:

print (<variable>)

Example:

X = 6

Y = 73

Name = "Tom"

print(X)

print(Y)

print(Name)

Here is a small R script which assigns values to variables using all 3 assignment operators and displays them one by one using the print function:

```
#Short demo on variables and assignment

#Assign some values to variables

#Equal to operator
FirstName = "Jackie"
#Leftward operator
LastName <- "Campbell"
#Rightward operator
28 -> Age

#Display all variables one by one using print
```

```
print (FirstName)
print (LastName)
print (Age)
```

Output:

```
F:\>cd R
F:\R>Rscript variables_1.r
[1] "Jackie"
[1] "Campbell"
[1] 28
F:\R>
```

As seen, the usage of print function is limited. You can only display one variable at a time. Also, there is no way of displaying descriptive text alongside variables such as – "First Name: Jackie". To address this shortcoming, there is a function called *cat( )*. This function can display multiple items at a time. An item can be a variable, constant or an expression. General syntax:

cat (item 1, item 2, ... item n)
Example:
name: "Xing"
country: "China"
cat ("Name: ", name , "Country: ", country)

If you want to display something on the next line, you can use the escape character sequence *"\n"* anywhere in a string constant or as a separate item perhaps at the end.

Here is an R script which makes use of the *cat* function to display variables in a meaningful manner:

7. Variables

```
#Variables Demo 2

#Assign some values to variables

First_Name = "Julio"
Last_Name = "Hernandez"
Age <- 34
"Mexico" -> Country

#Display everything using cat function

cat("First Name: ", First_Name, "\nLast Name: ",
Last_Name, "\nAge: ", Age, "\nCountry: ", Country,
"\n")
```

Output:

```
F:\R>Rscript variables_2.r
First Name:  Julio
Last Name:  Hernandez
Age:  34
Country:  Mexico

F:\R>_
```

7.3 Data Type of a Variable

A data type of a variable can be determined using the *class* function or the *typeof* function. The syntax of both these functions is as follows:

class (<variable>)

typeof(<variable>)

Example:

x = 3 + 5i

phone_brand = "Oppo"

print (class(x))

print (typeof(phone_brand))

27

8. Operators

An operator is a symbol or a group of symbols that performs a computational task. A computational task could be anything such as arithmetic operations, logical operations, comparison operations, etc. We have already seen 3 types of assignment operators which are used to assign values to variables. In this section we will learn more about other operators. R offers ***arithmetic operators, logical operators, relational operators and assignment operators***. We will cover each one of these categories in detail. There are some operators which do not fall under any particular category and will be covered as and when required. Some operators work better on ***Vectors*** and hence those will be covered in the ***Vectors*** chapter.

8.1 Arithmetic Operators

Arithmetic operators are used to perform arithmetic (or mathematical) operations such as addition, subtraction, multiplication, etc.

Operator	Description	Sample Usage	Explanation
+	Addition	x + y	Adds the given operands, returns sum of the operands.
-	Subtraction	x - y	Subtracts the operand on the right from the one on the left, returns difference of the operands.
*	Multiplication	x * y	Multiplies operands and returns the product.
/	Division	x / y	Performs division and returns the quotient.
%%	Modulus	x %% y	Performs division and returns the remainder.
%/%	Integer Division	x %/% y	Performs, integer division and returns the quotient in integer form only. For example, if we divide 5 by 2, the quotient is 2.5. However, if we perform integer division like this –> 5 %/% 2, we will get the quotient as 2.
^	Exponent	x ^ y	Raises the power of the operand on the left by the operand on the right. For example, 2 ^ 5 will give us 32.

8. Operators

Here is a simple script that demonstrate the usage of all arithmetic operators on two operands:

```
#Demo on Arithmetic Operators
#Declare two variables, assign some values
a = 125
b = 78
#Perform Arithmetic operations, assign result to variables
#Calculate sum
sum = a + b
#Calculate difference
difference = a - b
#Calculate product
product = a * b
#Perform division
quotient = a / b
#Find remainder
mod = a %% b
#Perform integer division
int_quotient = a %/% b
#Exponent
expo = a ^ b
#Display everything
cat(" a = ", a , "b = ", b, "\n",
    "sum = ", sum , "\n",
    "difference = ", difference , "\n",
    "product = ", product , "\n",
    "quotient = ", quotient , "\n",
    "remainder = ", mod , "\n",
    "quotient (integer) = ", int_quotient , "\n",
    "exponent = ", expo , "\n"
)
```

Output:

```
F:\R>Rscript arithmetic_operators.r
 a =  125 b = 78
 sum = 203
 difference = 47
 product = 9750
 quotient = 1.602564
 remainder = 47
 quotient (integer) = 1
 exponent = 3.622272e+163

F:\R>
```

8.2 Relational Operators

Relational Operators are used to compare operands. That is, determine if an operand is less than or greater than the other operand, whether an operand is equal to the other one and so son. These operators return **_TRUE_** or **_FALSE_**. In R, 0 is considered as **_FALSE_** and non-zero numbers including negative numbers are considered as **_TRUE_**. Relational operators are extensively used in control structures.

Operator	Description	Sample Usage	Explanation
==	Equal To	x == y	Returns TRUE if the values of the operands are equal, FALSE otherwise.
!=	Not Equal To	x != y	Returns TRUE if the values of the operands are not equal, FALSE otherwise.
<	Less Than	x < y	Returns TRUE if the value of the left operand is less than the value of the operand on the right, FALSE otherwise.
>	Greater Than	x > y	Returns TRUE if the value of the left operand is greater than the value of the operand on the right, FALSE otherwise.
<=	Less Than OR Equal To	x <= y	Returns TRUE if the value of the left operand is less than **_OR equal to_** the value of the operand on the right, FALSE otherwise.
>=	Greater Than OR Equal To	x >= y	Returns TRUE if the value of the left operand is greater than **_OR equal to_** the value of the operand on the right, FALSE otherwise.

Following is an R script where there are two variables. The usage of each of the above mentioned relational operators is demonstrated on the variables:

```
#Demo on Relational Operators
#Declare two variables, assign some values
a = 10
b = 20
#Perform Relational Operations and display directly
using cat function
cat(" a = ", a , "b = ", b, "\n",
    "a == b : ", a == b , "\n",
    "a != b : ", a != b , "\n",
    "a < b : ", a < b , "\n",
    "a > b : ", a > b , "\n",
    "a <= b : ", a <= b , "\n",
    "a >= b : ", a >= b , "\n"
)
```

Output:

```
F:\R>Rscript relational_operators.r
 a = 10 b = 20
 a == b : FALSE
 a != b : TRUE
 a < b : TRUE
 a > b : FALSE
 a <= b : TRUE
 a >= b : FALSE
F:\R>
```

8.3 Logical Operators

Logical operators are used to perform logical operations namely logical *OR, AND and NOT*. Result of these operations is either *TRUE* or *FALSE*.

Operator	Description	Sample Usage	Explanation
||	Logical OR	x || y	Compares operands and returns TRUE if any one of the values is non-zero, returns FALSE otherwise.
&&	Logical AND	x && y	Compares operands and returns TRUE if all the values are non-zero, returns FALSE otherwise.
!	Logical NOT	!x	Returns inverted value of the operand in logical form. If the operand has a TRUE value (non-zero), FALSE will be returned and if the operand has FALSE value (0), TRUE will be returned.

There are variations of *Logical OR* and *Logical AND* called *Elementwise OR (|)* and *Elementwise AND (&)*. The difference between these variations can only be understood using vectors and hence they are covered in the *Vectors* chapter.

Here is a script that demonstrate the usage of logical operators:

```
#Demo on Logical Operators

#Declare two variables, assign some values
a = 0
b = -6
#Use Logical Variables.
x = TRUE
y = FALSE

#Perform Logical Operations and display everything.
cat(" a = ", a , "b = ", b, "\n",
    "a && b : ", a && b , "\n",
    "a || b : ", a || b , "\n",
    "!a = ", !a , "\n",
    "!b = ", !b , "\n")
```

8. Operators

```
"\nUsing Logical Values:\n",
"x = ", x , "y = ", y, "\n",
"x && y : ", x && y , "\n",
"x || y : ", x || y , "\n",
"!x = ", !x , "\n",
"!y = ", !y , "\n"
)
```

Output:

8.4 Assignment Operators

Assignment operators are used to assign values to variables.

Operator(s)	Description	Sample Usage	Explanation
= , <- , <<-	Leftwards assignment operator	A = 5 B <- A + 9.6 Word <<- "Hello"	Assigns to the variable on the left the value of the operand on the right. If the operand on the right is an expression, it will be evaluated first and then assigned.
-> , ->>	Rightwards assignment operator	78.45 -> X -5 ->> Y	Assigns to the variable on the right, the value of the operand on the left. If the operand on the left is an expression, it will be evaluated first and then assigned.

35

The leftwards operators = and <- can be used interchangeably. When there is an R environment within another environment, the operator <<- is used for global assignments. This is a fairly advanced topic and you need not pay attention to it as a beginner. Rightwards assignment operators will work perfectly fine, but are not used very often.

9. R Terminal

R Terminal (also called *Rterm*) is a utility provided by the R distribution which allows developers to interact with the R interpreter. This utility is very useful and can be used for testing, debugging and rapid prototyping. Whatever R programming constructs you have learned can be tried out inside the R Terminal. Open *Command Prompt* on Windows or *Terminal/Shell* on MAC/Linux, type *R* and hit *Enter* to launch the *R Terminal*. You should see something like this:

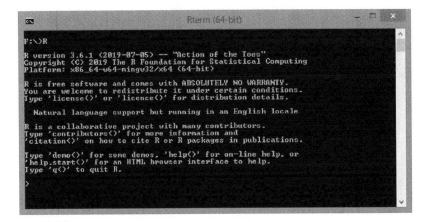

You can enter any valid R statements in this terminal and they will be executed in real time. For example, let us assign values to variables and perform arithmetic operations on them as follows:

a = 2.6
b = 7.9
c = 4.713
a + b + c
a − b * c
c / a
b ^ a

a * c %% b

a

b

c

Here's what we see after executing each of these statements:

```
Rterm (64-bit)

Type 'demo()' for some demos, 'help()' for on-line help, or
'help.start()' for an HTML browser interface to help.
Type 'q()' to quit R.

> a = 2.6
> b = 7.9
> c = 4.713
> a + b + c
[1] 15.213
> a - b * c
[1] -34.6327
> c / a
[1] 1.812692
> b ^ a
[1] 215.6902
> a * c %% b
[1] 12.2538
> a
[1] 2.6
> b
[1] 7.9
> c
[1] 4.713
>
```

If you want to quit R Terminal, type *q()* and hit **Enter**. You will be given an option to save **Workspace** image and you can choose *y (Yes), n (No), c (Cancel)*. The R Terminal will quit with *y* and *n* option; the quit procedure will be cancelled with the *c* option and you will return back to the normal R Terminal. If you chose to save the workspace with the *y* option, your work will be saved. Meaning, all the objects such as variables that you have used in that particular session will be saved and the next time you open R Terminal again, those variables will retain their previous values.

Whenever you are learning R or writing a script, I suggest you keep the R Terminal open so that you can try R statements inside the terminal and see how they work then and there. This will not be so straight forward with every R programming construct (such as control structures) but will work well with most.

10. User Input

Whatever programs we learned so far were hardcoded and did not involve any user interaction. In this section, we will learn how to accept input from the user. We will be using a built-in function called *readLines* which will serve this purpose. This function does a *blocking I/O operation* when configured with the appropriate options. That is, when the execution control encounters the *readLines* function, the program will wait for the user to enter something through the keyboard (and press *Enter*). If the user does not enter anything, the execution will halt and the program will stay there indefinitely until it is externally terminated. When the user enters something and presses *Enter*, the entered text will be fetched and returned. There must be a variable to receive the returned value. If there is no variable to catch the returned value, the function will work just fine but whatever the user has entered will be lost. The general syntax of using the *readLines* function is:

[variable] = *readLines* ("stdin", n = 1)
   OR
[variable] <- *readLines* ("stdin", n = 1)
Example:
cat ("Enter your name: ")
Name = *readLines* ("stdin", n = 1)

In the above example, the *readLines* function will prompt the user to enter the name and will wait for the input. Once the user enters something and presses *Enter*, it will be stored in the *Name* variable.

Let us write a program where we will prompt the user to enter name, city and country; store in 3 different variables and display using the cat function:

```
#User Input Demo
#Using readLines function to read user input

#Name
cat("\n Enter your name: ")
name <- readLines("stdin", n = 1)
#City
cat("\n Enter your city: ")
city <- readLines("stdin", n = 1)
#Country
cat("\n Enter your country: ")
country <- readLines("stdin", n = 1)

cat("\n Name: ", name, "\n",
    "City: ", city, "\n",
    "Country: ", country, "\n\n")
```

Output:

```
F:\R>Rscript user_input_1.r
Enter your name: Janice
Enter your city: Oslo
Enter your country: Norway

 Name:    Janice
 City:    Oslo
 Country: Norway

F:\R>
```

The *readLines* function is designed to read multiple lines either from a file or a keyboard. If you notice the syntax – *readLines* ("stdin", n = 1), "stdin" stands for standard input device (which is keyboard in most cases) and *n = 1* means *1* line is to be read.

The data type of the value returned by the *readLines* function will always be string/character even if the user enters a number.

10. User Input

When dealing with data types other than strings, the appropriate conversion functions should be used. Some of the useful conversion functions are as follows:

- **Character to Integer**
  - as.integer(<string>)
  - Example:
    - a = "5"
    - x = as.integer(a)
- **Character to Numeric**
  - as.numeric(<string>)
  - Example:
    - a = "347.353"
    - x = as.numeric(a)
- **Character to Complex**
  - as.complex(<string>)
  - Example:
    - a = "3 + 5i"
    - x = as.complex(a)

Let us write a script to calculate the area of a triangle using the following formula:

Area = ½ x Base x Height

We will ask the user to enter the base and the height of a triangle, read these values using *readLines* function, convert them to numeric and calculate the area.

```
#Area of a Triangle
#Using readLines function to read user input
#Using as.numeric to convert string to numeric

#Base
cat("\n Enter the base: ")
input_base <- readLines("stdin", n = 1)
#Height
cat("\n Enter the height: ")
input_height <- readLines("stdin", n = 1)

#Convert input_base and input_height to numeric
Base = as.numeric(input_base)
Height = as.numeric(input_height)
#Calculate area
Area = (1/2) * Base * Height

#Display Area
cat("\n Area: ", Area, "\n")
```

Output:

```
F:\R>Rscript area_triangle.r
Enter the base: 20
Enter the height: 10
Area: 100
F:\R>
```

At this point, it is recommended that you accept different kinds of inputs from the user, convert them to the appropriate formats if needed and perform various computations. This will sharpen your concepts and make you ready for the upcoming sections.

10. User Input

When dealing with data types other than strings, the appropriate conversion functions should be used. Some of the useful conversion functions are as follows:

- **Character to Integer**
  - *as.integer(<string>)*
  - *Example:*
    - *a = "5"*
    - *x = as.integer(a)*

- **Character to Numeric**
  - *as.numeric(<string>)*
  - *Example:*
    - *a = "347.353"*
    - *x = as.numeric(a)*

- **Character to Complex**
  - *as.complex(<string>)*
  - *Example:*
    - *a = "3 + 5i"*
    - *x = as.complex(a)*

Let us write a script to calculate the area of a triangle using the following formula:

Area = ½ x Base x Height

We will ask the user to enter the base and the height of a triangle, read these values using *readLines* function, convert them to numeric and calculate the area.

```r
#Area of a Triangle
#Using readLines function to read user input
#Using as.numeric to convert string to numeric

#Base
cat("\n Enter the base: ")
input_base <- readLines("stdin", n = 1)
#Height
cat("\n Enter the height: ")
input_height <- readLines("stdin", n = 1)

#Convert input_base and input_height to numeric
Base = as.numeric(input_base)
Height = as.numeric(input_height)
#Calculate area
Area = (1/2) * Base * Height

#Display Area
cat("\n Area: ", Area, "\n")
```

Output:

```
F:\R>Rscript area_triangle.r
Enter the base: 20
Enter the height: 10
Area: 100
F:\R>
```

At this point, it is recommended that you accept different kinds of inputs from the user, convert them to the appropriate formats if needed and perform various computations. This will sharpen your concepts and make you ready for the upcoming sections.

11. Vectors and Lists

11.1 Vectors

A vector is a basic data object in R and can contain elements of same or different data types. A vector containing elements of the same data type is known as an atomic vector. Atomic vectors can be of 6 basic data types – character, integer, double, complex, logical and raw.

11.1.1 Vector Creation

A vector can be created using the *c( )* function. General syntax:

<variable> = c(<elements separated by comma>)
Eg:
#Atomic vector of numeric type
x <- c(1, 2.6, 3.1)
#Atomic vector of character type (string)
countries <- c("Vietnam", "China", "Uzbekistan")
#Non-atomic vectors
data <- c(67, "Apple", 3 + 2i, "Colombo")

The length of a vector can be obtained using the *length* function as follows:

length (<vector>)
Eg:
x <- (1, 2, 3)
l = length (x)

A vector can be created by *filling it with consecutive numbers* as follows:

<variable> = <starting number> : <ending number>

Eg:

#Fill from 1 to 5

a = 1:5

If you want to fill a vector with a sequence having a custom step, you can use the *seq()* function as follows:

<variable> = seq(<start>, <end>, by = <step size>)

Eg:

#Fill from 1 to 5 with a step size of 0.5

x = seq(1, 5, by = 0.5)

Here is a small program that combines all these concepts:

```
#Vectors Demo

#Create a simple vector
x <- c(4,5,9)
#Display vector x
cat("\nVector x: ", x)
#Create another vector
y <- c("Intel", "AMD", 9.5, 1.675, "NVIDIA")
#Display vector y
cat("\nVector y: ", y)
#Fill 5 to -5 in vector z
z <- 5:-5
#Display vector z
cat("\nVector z: ", z)
#Create a vector with values from 8 to 12 with a step of 0.4
s <- seq(8, 12, by = 0.4)
#Display vector s
cat("\nVector s: ", s)
```

Output:

```
F:\R>Rscript vectors1.r
Vector x:  4 5 9
Vector y:  Intel AMD 9.5 1.675 NVIDIA
Vector z:  5 4 3 2 1 0 -1 -2 -3 -4 -5
Vector s:  8 8.4 8.8 9.2 9.6 10 10.4 10.8 11.2 11.6 12
F:\R>_
```

11.1.2 Accessing Vector Elements

An element of a vector can be accessed using its index. Indices start at 1 and end at the length of the vector. For example, if the length of a vector is 5, the first element will be present at 1 and the last element will be present at 5.

An element at index n can be accessed as:

<vector variable>[n]

Eg:

x = c(1, 2, 3)

elem = x[2]

You can even modify the element at that index using the same method. For example:

<vector variable>[n] = <value>

Eg:

x[3] = 30

If you want to access all elements except the element at a particular index, you can specify that index with a negative number. For example, consider a vector *V* with elements *(10, 20, 30, 40,*

50). If you want to access all elements but not the element at index 4, you can do it as follows – *V[-4]*.

It is possible to access more than one elements at a time using the following syntax:

> *<vector variable>[c(<indices separated by comma>)]*
>
> *Eg:*
>
> *x = c(9, 8, 7, 6, 5)*
>
> *#Return elements 1, 2 and 5. Assign to y as a new vector*
>
> *y = x[c(1, 2, 5)]*

Here is a simple R script that explains these concepts:

```
#Vectors Demo II

#Create a vector
x <- c(1.5,7.6,9.89,7.245,5.64,8.78)
#Display vector x
cat("\nVector x: ", x)
#Display element at index 5
cat("\nElement at index 5: ", x[5])
#Display elements at index 1, 2 and 4
cat("\nElement at index 1, 2, 4: ", x[c(1, 2, 4)])
#Modify elements at index 3 and 6
x[3] = 0
x[6] = 100
#Display x again
cat("\nVector x after modification: ", x)
```

Output:

```
F:\R>Rscript vectors2.r
Vector x:  1.5 7.6 9.89 7.245 5.64 8.78
Element at index 5:  5.64
Element at index 1, 2, 4:  1.5 7.6 7.245
Vector x after modification:  1.5 7.6 0 7.245 5.64 100
F:\R>
```

11.1.3 Vector Operations

All the operators mentioned in *Section 8* work on atomic vectors of numeric types. You can add, subtract, multiply, divide vectors, can compare two vectors, etc. The only condition here is; the vectors should be of the same length. The process is the same as you would use with any other variables or constants. Refer to the following code snippet which shows basic arithmetic operations on vectors:

V1 = c(1, 2, 3)
V2 = c(9, 8, 7)
#Arithmetic operations
Sum = V1 + V2
Diff = V1 – V2

When you perform arithmetic operations on two vectors, the result will also be a vector. For example, if you add *V1* and *V2* from the above code snippet, the result will be a vector bearing the elements *(10, 10, 10)*. When you use relational operators with vectors, the result will be an atomic vector of logical type. For example, consider these two vectors – *x (1, 5, 2)* and *y (2, 1, 6)*. If you want to check if *x* is less than *y* using the *(<)* operator like this – *(x < y)*, each element from *x* will be checked with the corresponding element from *y*. That is, the following operations will be implicitly performed – *(1 < 2), (5 < 1), (2 < 6)*. The result will be a logical vector having elements – *(TRUE, FALSE, TRUE)*.

The usage of *Logical Operators* with vectors is interesting. We have already studied *Logical AND (&&)* and *Logical OR (||)*. When using these operators with vectors, only the first element of each vector will be compared and the rest will be ignored. There are two more operators available which are known as *Elementwise Logical AND (&)* and *Elementwise Logical OR (|)*. When these operators are used with vectors, logical AND and OR operations are performed on <u>each element of the vectors</u>. Here is an R script which demonstrates the usage of all the operators on vectors:

```
#Declare two vectors, assign some values
a <- c(1, 0, 3)
b <- c(7, 2, -9)
#Perform Arithmetic operations, assign result to vector variable
#Calculate sum
sum = a + b
#Calculate difference
difference = a - b
#Calculate product
product = a * b
#Peform division
quotient = a / b
#Find remainder
mod = a %% b
#Perform integer division
int_quotient = a %/% b
#Exponent
expo = a ^ b
#Display everything
cat("Arithmetic Operators\n a = ", a , "b = ", b, "\n",
    "sum = ", sum , "\n",
    "difference = ", difference , "\n",
    "product = ", product , "\n",
    "quotient = ", quotient , "\n",
    "remainder = ", mod , "\n",
    "quotient (integer) = ", int_quotient , "\n",
    "exponent = ", expo , "\n"
    )
#Perform Relational Operations and display directly using cat function
cat("\n\nRelational Operators\n a = ", a , "b = ", b, "\n",
```

11. Vectors and Lists

```
    "a == b : ", a == b , "\n",
    "a != b : ", a != b , "\n",
    "a <  b : ", a <  b , "\n",
    "a >  b : ", a >  b , "\n",
    "a <= b : ", a <= b , "\n",
    "a >= b : ", a >= b , "\n"
)
#Perform Logical Operations and display everything.
cat("\n\nLogical Operators\n a = ", a , "b = ", b,
"\n",
    "a && b : ", a && b , "\n",
    "a || b : ", a || b , "\n",
    "a &  b : ", a &  b , "\n",
    "a |  b : ", a |  b , "\n",
    "!a = ", !a , "\n",
    "!b = ", !b , "\n"
)
```

Output:

```
F:\R>Rscript vector_operations.r
Arithmetic Operators
a =  1 0 3 b =  7 2 -9
sum =  8 2 -6
difference =  -6 -2 12
product =  7 0 -27
quotient =  0.1428571 0 -0.3333333
remainder =  1 0 -6
quotient (integer) =  0 0 -1
exponent =  1 0 5.080526e-05

Relational Operators
a =  1 0 3 b =  7 2 -9
a == b :  FALSE FALSE FALSE
a != b :  TRUE TRUE TRUE
a <  b :  TRUE TRUE FALSE
a >  b :  FALSE FALSE TRUE
a <= b :  TRUE TRUE FALSE
a >= b :  FALSE FALSE TRUE

Logical Operators
a =  1 0 3 b =  7 2 -9
a && b :  TRUE
a || b :  TRUE
a &  b :  TRUE FALSE TRUE
a |  b :  TRUE TRUE TRUE
!a =  FALSE TRUE FALSE
!b =  FALSE FALSE FALSE
F:\R>
```

11.2 Lists

A list is a combination of elements of any data type(s). A list can contain strings, numbers, vectors, etc. and even other lists.

11.2.1 List Creation

A list can be created using the *list()* function as follows:

<list variable> = list (<element 1>, <element 2>, ... <element n>)
Example:
random_list = list (40, "Joy", 5.8, c(1, 2, 3), "HK", 4 + 6i)

11.2.2 Accessing List Elements

An element of a list can be accessed using its index. Index of a list starts at 1 and ends at the length of the list. For example, if the length of a list is 6, the first element will be present at 1 and the last element will be present at 6.

An element at index *i* can be accessed as:

<list variable>[i]
Eg:
random_list = list (40, "Joy", 5.8, c(1, 2, 3), "HK", 4 + 6i)

From this example, the first element **40** can be accessed as **random_list[1]**, the second element **"Joy"** can be accessed as **random_list[2]** and so on... The last element **4 + 6i** can be accessed as **random_list[6]**.

11.2.3 Miscellaneous List Operations

- Two or more lists can be merged into a bigger list by creating a vector of individual lists. For example, if you have lists called **list1, list2 and list3**. You can merge these lists by creating a vector of these lists like this – **list4 <- c(list1, list2, list3)**.

11. Vectors and Lists

- The length of a list can be determined by the *length(<list>)* function.

- A list can be converted to a vector using the *unlist(<list>)* function.

- It can be determined whether or not a variable is a list by using the *is.list(<variable>)* function. This function returns **TRUE** if the variable is a list, returns **FALSE** otherwise.

Here is an R script that demonstrates different list operations:

```
#List Demo
#Create a list
list_1 = list (8.1, "Jonny", 4 + 7i )
#Display list_1
cat("\n\nlist_1:\n")
print (list_1)
cat("\nLength: ", length(list_1), "\nIs list_1 a list? ", is.list(list_1))
cat("\n\nChanging value at list_1[3] to 5.8\n")
list_1[3] = 5.8
print (list_1)
#Create another list
list_2 = list (c(1:5), "Peru")
#Display list_2
cat("\nlist_2:\n")
print (list_2)
cat("\nLength: ", length(list_2), "\nIs list_2 a list? ", is.list(list_2))
#Merge list_1 and list_2 into list_3
list_3 = c(list_1, list_2)
#Display list_3
cat("\n\nlist_3:\n")
print (list_3)
cat("\nLength: ", length(list_3), "\nIs list_1 a list? ", is.list(list_3))
#Convert list_3 to vector
v1 = unlist(list_3)
cat("\n\nVector v1:\n")
print (v1)
```

```
  cat("\nLength: ", length(v1), "\nIs v1 a list? ",
is.list(v1), "\nIs v1 a vector? ", is.vector(v1),
"\n\n")
```

Output (1):

```
F:\R>Rscript listdemo.r

list_1:
[[1]]
[1] 8.1

[[2]]
[1] "Jonny"

[[3]]
[1] 4+7i

Length:  3
Is list_1 a list?  TRUE
Changing value at list_1[3] to 5.8
[[1]]
[1] 8.1

[[2]]
[1] "Jonny"

[[3]]
[1] 5.8

list_2:
[[1]]
[1] 1 2 3 4 5

[[2]]
[1] "Peru"

Length:  2
Is list_2 a list?  TRUE
```

Output (2):

```
list_3:
[[1]]
[1] 8.1

[[2]]
[1] "Jonny"

[[3]]
[1] 5.8

[[4]]
[1] 1 2 3 4 5

[[5]]
[1] "Peru"

Length:  5
Is list_1 a list?  TRUE
Vector v1:
[1] "8.1"   "Jonny" "5.8"   "1"   "2"   "3"   "4"   "5"   "Peru"
Length:  9
Is v1 a list?  FALSE
Is v1 a vector?  TRUE
```

12. Control Structures

Control structures are programming constructs used to obtain better control over the execution of a program. Normally, a script would execute line by line following a top-to-bottom (or top-down) approach. This flow of execution can be altered using control structures. R offers decision making constructs and loops as control structures.

12.1 Decision making

Decision making constructs are available in the form of if-else statements and switch function.

12.1.1 if, else, else if Statements

Let us take a look at a simple *if* statement first. The usage of if statement is quite straight forward – <u>if a condition is true, then execute a block of code</u>. The general syntax for using an *if* statement is as follows:

```
if ( < expression > ) {
    #This is the if-block
    <statements...>
}
```

When an *if* statement is encountered, the specified *<expression>* is evaluated. This expression is a **Boolean expression** and can evaluate to *TRUE* or *FALSE*. It can be recalled that in addition to Boolean *TRUE* and *FALSE* values, all **non-zero** numbers are considered as *TRUE* and *0* is considered as *FALSE*. If the evaluation of the Boolean expression returns ***TRUE***, the statements inside the ***if-block*** are executed, a ***FALSE*** value will skip the execution of the ***if-block***. A block is enclosed within curly brackets ({ }). The ***if-block*** can be followed by an optional ***else-block*** which will get executed if the specified ***<expression>*** of the ***if-block*** is evaluated to ***FALSE***.

```
if ( < expression > ) {
        #This is the if-block
        #Executed when < expression > returns TRUE
        <statements...>
} else {
        #This is the else-block
        #Executed when < expression > returns FALSE
        <statements...>
}
```

Note: The ***else block*** should immediately follow the ***if block***. There can be no statements after the end of the ***if-block*** and just before the ***else*** statement.

It is also possible to nest if-else statements as follows:

```
if ( < expression 1 >) {
        #This block will be executed if < expression 1 > is TRUE.
        if ( < expression 2 > ) {
                #This block will be executed if < expression 1 >
                and < expression 2 > are TRUE.
                <statements...>
        } else {
```

```
                #This block will be executed if < expression 1 > is
                TRUE and <expression 2> is FALSE.
                <statements...>
            }
        } else {
            #This block will be executed if < expression 1 > is FALSE.
            if ( < expression 3 > ) {
                #This block will be executed if < expression 1 > is
                FALSE and < expression 3 > is TRUE.
                <statements...>
            }
        }
```

An *if* statement can only have one *else* statement. This means, you can only check for one condition if you do not consider using nested *if-else* statements. There is another part to *if-else* construct which lets you test for multiple condition. This is known as *else-if* construct. The *else-if* code block is not standalone and has to be a part of *if-else* construct. This is how it works – there will be a mandatory *if* statement with a supplied expression, multiple *else-if* statements <u>with their own expressions</u> and an optional *else* statement. The expression of the *if* statement will be checked first, if it evaluates to **_TRUE_**, the *if* block will be executed and rest of the blocks will be ignored. If the expression evaluates to **_FALSE_**, the expression of the immediate (next) *else-if* block will be checked. If that evaluates to **_TRUE_**, that particular block will be executed and rest of the blocks will be ignored. If that expression also evaluates to **_FALSE_**, the next *else if* block (if present) will be checked and this process will go on until a **_TRUE_** expression is found. If none of the expressions evaluate to *TRUE*, the *else* block (if present) will be executed. Check out the following code snippet that explains the use of *else-if* statements.

if (<expression 1>) {
    #This block will be executed if < expression 1 > is TRUE.
} else if (< expression 2>) {
    #This block will be executed if < expression 1 > is FALSE
< expression 2 > is TRUE.
<statements...>
} else if (< expression 3 >) {
    #This block will be executed if < expression 1 > and < expression 2 > are FALSE and < expression 3 > is TRUE.
<statements...>
} else {
    #This block will be executed if < expression 1 >, < expression 2 > and   < expression 3 > are FALSE.
}

Let us write a simple R script to accept a number from the user as an input and check if it is positive, negative or zero. Here is the script:

```
#If Else Else If Demo

#Read a number. readLines will return string data
cat("\n Enter a number: ")
num_str <- readLines("stdin", n = 1)
#Convert the read number from string to numeric form
num = as.numeric(num_str)
#Check if +ve, -ve or 0
if (num > 0) {
    #If num is greater than 0, it is positive
    cat("\nThe number: ", num, " is positive.\n")

#If num is less than 0, it is negative
```

12. Control Structures

```
} else if (num < 0) {
    cat("\nThe number: ", num, " is negative.\n")

} else {
    #If num is neither positive nor negative, means it
    is 0
    cat("\nThe number: ", num, " is zero.\n")
}
```

Output:

```
F:\R>Rscript if_else_demo.r
Enter a number: -573.46
The number:  -573.46  is negative.
F:\R>Rscript if_else_demo.r
Enter a number: 0
The number:  0  is zero.
F:\R>Rscript if_else_demo.r
Enter a number: 863
The number:  863  is positive.
F:\R>
```

Note: It is important to note the syntax and semantics of *if-else, else if* construct. Wherever an *if* or an *else if* block ends, marked by a closing curly bracket (}), the following *else if* or *else* statement should be present on the same line. For example, the following code snipped is semantically incorrect because the else statement is not present on the same line where the if block ends:

if (< expression >) {
}
else {
}

The same snippet can be correctly written as follows:

> *if (< expression >) {*
> *} else {*
> *}*

12.1.2 switch Function

In many trivial programming languages such as C/C++, Python, Java, there is a decision making construct called **switch** which helps in making a decision when an expression can lead to multiple outcomes. This saves the trouble to writing several *if, else if* and *else* statements, perhaps nested ones. In R, **switch** is available as a function and it returns a value. This function does pretty much the same job as compared to **switch** construct from other programming languages but the working is slightly different.

In R, **switch** is used to <u>test an expression against a list of elements</u>. General Syntax:

> *switch (<expression>, <list of elements separated by comma>)*
> *Eg:*
> *switch (2, "Motorola", "Alcatel", "LG")*

First, the expression is evaluated. Let us consider the expression evaluates to a number. This number is used to select the element according to its serial number. If the number is less than 0 or greater than the number of elements in the list, **NULL** is returned (i.e. No element is returned). Let us consider that there are three elements in the list. The simplified syntax would look like:

> *swtich (<expression>, <element 1>, <element 2>, <element 3>)*

12. Control Structures

If the *<expression>* evaluates to *1*, *<element 1>* will be returned. If it evaluates to *2*, *<element 2>* will be returned and if it evaluates to *3*, *<element 3>* will be returned. An evaluation to any number less than *1* or greater than *3* (total number of elements in the list) will result in the value being returned as **NULL**.

Here is a code snippet of switch examples being run inside the R terminal:

#Select 1 from list of 2
switch (1, "USA", "CANADA")
#Select 0 from list of 2, NULL
switch (0, "Oppo", "Vivo")
#Select 5 from list of 4, NULL
switch (5, "Lenovo", "HP", "Dell", "MSI")
#Select 3 from list of 3
switch (3, "Audi", "BMW", "Jaguar")

Output (R Terminal):

```
R version 3.6.1 (2019-07-05) -- "Action of the Toes"
Copyright (C) 2019 The R Foundation for Statistical Computing
Platform: x86_64-w64-mingw32/x64 (64-bit)

R is free software and comes with ABSOLUTELY NO WARRANTY.
You are welcome to redistribute it under certain conditions.
Type 'license()' or 'licence()' for distribution details.

  Natural language support but running in an English locale

R is a collaborative project with many contributors.
Type 'contributors()' for more information and
'citation()' on how to cite R or R packages in publications.

Type 'demo()' for some demos, 'help()' for on-line help, or
'help.start()' for an HTML browser interface to help.
Type 'q()' to quit R.

> switch (1, "USA", "CANADA")
[1] "USA"
> switch (0, "Oppo", "Vivo")
> switch (5, "Lenovo", "HP", "Dell", "MSI")
> switch (3, "Audi", "BMW", "Jaguar")
[1] "Jaguar"
>
```

Note: This is a very simple example which shows the working of *switch*. There is a lot you can do with it. For example, execute a block of code when a matching element is found. This is covered in the *Functions* chapter of this book.

12.2 Loops

Loops are programming constructs used to run a piece of code over and over again. R offers 3 loops – *while loop, repeat loop and for loop.* We will be looking at each one of these.

12.2.1 while Loop

A while loop is used to execute a block of code until a condition is met. The specified condition is normally a Boolean expression and should evaluate to *TRUE* or *FALSE*. Syntax:

while (<condition>) {
    #Statements...
    ...
    ...
}

When the *while* loop is encountered, the specified condition is checked. If it evaluates to *TRUE*, the statements inside the while block are executed one by one. The process where the set of statements get executed one by one starting from the first statement until the end of the block is known as a *loop iteration*. When the execution control reaches the end of the block, the condition is checked again and if it evaluates to *TRUE* again, the block of code is executed again. This process goes on as long as the specified condition evaluates to *TRUE*. If it evaluates to *FALSE*, the block of code will not be executed. If the condition never evaluates to *FALSE*, the loop will go on executing; such a loop is known as an *infinite loop*.

Consider the following code snippet where we display numbers from 1 to 10 using a *while* loop:

```
#Initiate a variable to 1, that's where we start our count from
Number <- 1
#Loop until Number is 10
while ( Number <= 10 ) {
    #Display Number
    print (Number)
    #Increment Number by 1
    Number = Number + 1
}
```

12.2.2 for Loop

The *for* Loop is more efficient loop and can be used when you need to execute a block of code for a specific number of iterations. General Syntax:

```
for ( <value> in <list/vector>) {
    #Statements…
    …
    …
}
```

This loop needs a list or a vector to execute. The number of elements in the vector will be equal to the number of times this loops execute. During each iteration, an element from the vector will be fetched in the **<value>** variable. During next iteration, the next element will be fetched and this process will go on until the last element is fetched. The vector need not be an atomic one or necessarily contain numbers, elements of any data type will work just fine. Here is a code snipped to display 1 to 10 using for loop. We will be using (:) operator to fill a vector first and use the for loop to display them one by one.

```
#Fill x with 1 to 10
x <- 1:10
#Run for loop for as many number of times as the number of elements in x
for (val in x) {
    #Display val
    print (val)
}
```

12.2.3 Loop Control

Before we move on to the **repeat** loop, we need to understand loop control. A **while** loop will normally go on executing as long as the given condition is met and a **for** loop will go on executing as long as the elements in the given list have been iterated through. If you want to alter this normal process of loop execution, you can use loop control statements. R offers two loop control statements – **break** and **next**. When break statement is encountered, the execution of the loop will stop and the control will come out of the loop. Whereas, when **next** statement is encountered, the current iteration is skipped thereby ignoring all the statements after the **next** statement inside the loop block and the execution control goes to the beginning of the loop. In case of a ***while*** loop, the next iteration will begin by checking the condition and if it evaluates to ***TRUE***, the execution of the loop block will begin from the first statement. In case of a ***for*** loop, the next element from the list will be fetched and then the execution will begin from the first statement of the loop block.

12.2.4 repeat Loop

There is not termination condition for the ***repeat*** loop and it will go on executing indefinitely. The only way to terminate the execution of this loop is using the ***break*** statement. General Syntax:

```
repeat {
    #Statements...
    ...
    ...
}
```

It is ideal to check for a condition manually inside the loop and terminate using the ***break*** statement. This is how the syntax would look:

```
repeat {
    #Statements...
    ...
    ...
    if (<condition>) {
        break
    }
}
```

Consider the following code snippet where we display numbers from 1 to 10 using a *repeat* loop. We terminate it manually using a break statement when value reaches 11:

```
#Initiate a variable to 1, that's where we start our count from
Number <- 1
#Run indefinitely
repeat {
        #Display Number
        print (Number)
        #Increment Number by 1
        Number = Number + 1
        if ( Number == 11 ) {
                #Come out of the loop when Number reaches 11
                break
        }
}
```

Go through the following R script that demonstrates the usage of different loops and control statements:

```
#Loop Demo

#Display multiples of 5 using while loop
i = 1
#Run while until i becomes 10
cat("\nMultiples of 5: \n")
while ( i <= 10 ) {
   cat(5 * i, " ")
   i = i + 1
   }
#Create vector from -3 to 6 with a step of 0.5
x = seq(-3, 6, by = 0.5)
cat("\n\nVector x: \n", x)
#Iterate through x using for loop and find the sum of
all the elements
s = 0
```

12. Control Structures

```r
for (val in x) {
   s = s + val
   }
cat("\n\nSum of all elements of x: ", s)
#Display 1 to 5 using repeat loop, break when value reaches 5
cat("\n\nDisplaying 1 to 5 using repeat loop.\n")
j = 1
repeat {
   cat (j, " ")
   j = j + 1
   if ( j == 6 ) {
        break
        }
   }
#Display multiples of 2 using while loop, but skip when the value is also a multiple of 3
i = 1
#Run while until i becomes 10
cat("\nMultiples of 2 (and not of 3): \n")
while ( i <= 10 ) {
   multiple = i * 2
   i = i + 1
   #Skip when also a multiple of 3
   if (( multiple %% 3) == 0) {
        next
        }
   cat(multiple, " ")
   }
```

Output:

```
F:\R>Rscript loopdemo.r
Multiples of 5:
5  10  15  20  25  30  35  40  45  50
Vector x:
-3 -2.5 -2 -1.5 -1 -0.5 0 0.5 1 1.5 2 2.5 3 3.5 4 4.5 5 5.5 6
Sum of all elements of x:  28.5
Displaying 1 to 5 using repeat loop.
1 2 3 4 5
Multiples of 2 (and not of 3):
2  4  8  10  14  16  20
F:\R>_
```

13. Functions

A function is a block of code that carries out a certain task or a set of tasks. Functions are also known as methods, routines or sub-routines. One of the primary reasons why functions exist is to avoid writing the same code again and again, thereby promoting code reusability. We have already seen built-in functions such as *print, cat, seq*, etc. Someone has already written code for the *print* function which we all can use to display something on the screen. Imagine what it would be like if we had to write code to interact with the output stream of the device every time we wanted to display a simple message on the screen. In this section, we will learn to write our own functions.

The topic of functions can be classified into two parts – *Function Definition* and *Function Call*.

13.1 Function Definition

A function definition has four distinct parts – function name, list of arguments (optional), function body and return value (optional).

Function Name

Function name is a name given to a function in order to uniquely identify it. The rules of naming a function are the same as the rules of naming a variable.

List of Arguments

A function can optionally accept variables to carry out work. These arguments are received in local variables. Arguments are also known as parameters.

Function Body

This is the part of a function where the actual work gets done. A function body comprises of a set of statements.

Return Value

A function can optionally return a value back to the calling function.

The general syntax of function definition is:

[function name] <- function (<arguments separated by comma>) {
  #Function Body
  #Statements…
    …
}

Following are a few examples of function definitions:

A function that does not accept any arguments and does not return any value:

myFunction <- function () {
  print ("Inside myFunction!")
}

A function that accepts 3 arguments and does not return any value:

demoFunction <- function (a, b, c) {
  cat ("a = ", a , "b = ", b , "c = ", c)
}

13. Functions

A function that accepts 3 arguments and returns the sum:

```
sumFunction <- function (a, b, c) {
    sum = a + b + c
    return (sum)
}
```

Note: Although functions can be written anywhere in the program, it is ideal to write them at the beginning of the script.

13.2 Function Call

A function when defined does not execute on its own and sits idle unless called. If a function is defined and never called, that piece of code will be pretty much useless. The general syntax of calling a function is:

<function name> (<list of arguments>)

Recall the *myFunction* definition from the previous section, this is how you would call it:

myFunction ( )

Let us recall *demoFunction* definition from the previous section. It accepts 3 arguments and hence, 3 values have to be passed as parameters while calling the function as follows:

demoFunction (1, 4, 7)

Note that the number of arguments in the function definition and in the function call should be exactly the same (unless using default arguments). Also, the arguments are received in the order that they are passed during function call. In the case of this function call – *demoFunction (1, 4, 7)*, *a* will receive *1*, *b* will receive *4* and *c* will receive *7*.

A function that returns a value should be called as follows:

<variable> = <function name> (<list of arguments>)

When a function returns a value, there should be a variable in the calling function to receive the returned value. Without it, the function should work just fine but the returned value will be lost and the process may be meaningless at times. For example, if you have written a function to calculate average of some numbers, you call the function, return the average but fail to receive the returned value; there is no point in going through the whole process in such a case.

Recall the **sumFunction** definition which accepts 3 values and returns their sum. This is how you would call it:

S = sumFunction (4.7, 87.3, 9)

When this function call is made, *4.7* will be received by *a*, *87.3* will be received by *b* and *9* will be received by *c*. Sum of these 3 values will be calculated and returned back to the calling function. The variable *S* will receive the returned value.

It is also possible to specify the argument names while calling a function. This way, the arguments need not be in order as defined in the function definition. For example:

S = sumFunction (b = 6, a = 9, c = 1)

13. Functions

Let us write an R script to demonstrate different kinds of functions:

```r
#Functions Demo
#A function that does not accept any arguments, does not return any value

simpleFunction <- function() {
    #Display a simple message
    cat("\n\nInside simpleFunction.\n")
}
#A function that accepts 3 arguments but does not return any value
displayData <- function(name, address, age) {
    #Display received data
    cat("\n\nInside displayData.\n
        \nName: ", name, "\nAddress: ", address,
        "\nAge: ", age)
}
#A function that accepts 3 arguments and returns their sum
findSum <- function(x, y, z) {
    cat("\n\nInside findSum.\n")
    #Calculate sum
    s = x + y + z
    #Return s
    return (s)
}
#Call each of these functions one by one
cat("\nCalling simpleFunction.")
simpleFunction()
cat("\nCalling displayData.")
#Call displayData, pass 3 values
displayData("Isabel", "Chicago", 29)
#Call findSum, pass 3 numeric values
cat("\n\nCalling findSum.")
s = findSum(5.8, 8.9, 1.2)
cat("\nOutside findSum; Sum = ", s, "\n\n")
```

Output:

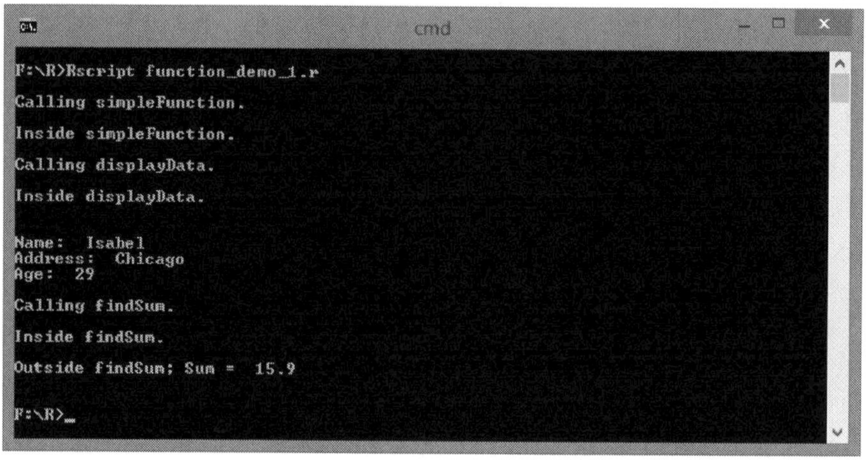

```
F:\R>Rscript function_demo_1.r
Calling simpleFunction.
Inside simpleFunction.
Calling displayData.
Inside displayData.

Name:    Isabel
Address: Chicago
Age:     29
Calling findSum.
Inside findSum.
Outside findSum; Sum =  15.9

F:\R>_
```

Note: R is an interpreted language and hence statements of an R script are executed starting from the first statement till the last one. This is what we have learned. If you notice the previous coding example, after the first few comments, ***simpleFunction*** is present. This being effectively the first line of code, does not get executed. This is because, the function code remains inactive until called. If many functions are present in a script, they all will be ignored at first and executed only when called. Refer to the following screenshot of the above R script. The exact place where execution begins has been marked.

13. Functions

```
1   #Functions Demo
2   #A function that does not accept any arguments, does not return any value
3
4   simpleFunction <- function() {       ⬅ Execution Does not begin here!
5       #Display a simple message
6       cat("\n\nInside simpleFunction.\n")
7   }
8   #A function that accepts 3 arguments but does not return any value
9   displayData <- function(name, address, age) {
10      #Display received data
11      cat("\n\nInside displayData.\n",
12          "\nName: ", name, "\nAddress: ", address,
13          "\nAge: ", age)
14  }
15  #A function that accepts 3 arguments and returns their sum
16  findSum <- function(x, y, z) {
17      cat("\n\nInside findSum.\n")
18      #Calculate sum
19      s = x + y + z
20      #Return s
21      return (s)
22  }
23  #Call each of these functions one by one
24  cat("\nCalling simpleFunction.")       ⬅ Execution starts here!
25  simpleFunction()
26  cat("\nCalling displayData.")
27  #Call displayData, pass 3 values
28  displayData("Isabel", "Chicago", 29)
29  #Call findSum, pass 3 numeric values
30  cat("\n\nCalling findSum.")
31  s = findSum(5.8, 8.9, 1.2)
32  cat("\nOutside findSum; Sum = ", s, "\n\n")
33
```

13.3 Default Arguments

Arguments can be given default values. When calling a function, if no arguments are passed, the default values will be considered (if it is set). General Syntax:

[function name] <- *function (<arg 1> = <value 1>, … <arg n> = <value n>)* {

    #Statements…

    …

}

Eg:

findProduct <- function (a, b, c = 1) {

    *product = a * b * c*

    print (product)

}

In this example, there is a function called ***findProduct*** which has two mandatory arguments – ***a*** and ***b*** and a default argument ***c***. While calling this function, only two arguments need to be passed and the third one will be taken as *1*. If the third argument is passed, the passed value will override the default value.

Note: Default arguments should always be at the end.

13.4 Nested Function Calls

It is possible to call one function from another and also possible nest a function call within another function call. Consider we have the following definition of ***findSum*** function which accepts 3 values and returns their sum:

```
findSum <- function (x, y, z) {
    return (x + y + z)
}
```

Example of nesting – If you want to display the sum using this function, you have two options. Call ***findSum*** function and receive the returned value in a variable and display that variable or embed the call to the ***findSum*** function within the ***cat*** function itself as follows:

```
cat ("Sum: " , findSum(1, 2, 3))
```

The value returned by ***findSum*** function will be directly substituted.

13.5 Using switch() function effectively

The switch function is an important decision making construct. It can be used to make an appropriate function call based on what the given expression evaluates to. Let us write a program to accept a number from the user and check if it is odd or even:

13. Functions

```r
#Function to display odd or even
displayResult <- function (num, result) {
    cat("\nThe number: ", num, " is ", result)
}
#Ask the user to enter a number
cat("\n Enter a number: ")
n <- readLines("stdin", n = 1)
#Convert to integer
num = as.integer(n)
#Check odd or even by performing num %% 2
odd_or_even = num %% 2
#If odd_or_even is 0, num is even else it is odd
#Use switch to make appropriate call to displayResult
switch((odd_or_even + 1), displayResult(num, "EVEN"),
displayResult(num, "ODD"))
```

Output:

```
F:\R>Rscript oddoreven.r
Enter a number: 125

The number:  125  is  ODD
F:\R>Rscript oddoreven.r
Enter a number: 86

The number:  86  is  EVEN
F:\R>
```

14. Strings

A string is a sequence of individual characters. In R, strings belong to the character data type. We have seen plenty of string examples this far. In this chapter, we will revise the concepts that we already know and also learn few more things about strings.

14.1 String Formation

A string can be formed by enclosing the group of characters within single quotes or double quotes like this:

String_1 <- 'Hi, this is a string'
   #OR
String_2 <- "This is also a string"

It is not possible to start a string with a single quote and end with a double quote or vice-versa.

If you want to include a single quote as a part of the string, you need to enclose the string within double quotes and if you want to include a double quote as a part of the string you need to enclose the string within single quotes.

14.2 String Concatenation

Two or more strings can be concatenated using the paste function. The syntax of *paste* function according to its definition is as follows:

paste (<strings>, sep = <separator>, collapse = NULL)
Where:
<strings> - is a group of strings to be concatenated, separated by comma.
<separator> - is the character used to separate two consecutive strings.

collapse - is the argument used to remove space between two strings (but between a string.

Example:
S1 = "This"
S2 = "is"
S3 = "an R eBook"
New_str = paste (S1, S2, S3, sep = " ", collapse = "")

The paste function will return a new string which will be a concatenation of the given strings.

14.3 Substring

A substring is a subset of a larger string. For example, if we have a string – **"R is a great scripting language!"**, we can clearly see that **"is a great"** is a part of this string and hence can be called as a substring. Of course, there are many more substring examples here. In order to extract a substring from a string, we can use a function called substring. General Syntax:

substring (<source string>, <start position>, <end position>)

This function will return a string which is a substring of the **<source string>**.

Here is an R script that demonstrates concatenation and substring concepts:

```
#String Concatenation Demo
#Declare 3 strings
str1 = "World"
str2 = "is a"
str3 = "beautiful place!!!"
#Concatenate using space
concat1 = paste(str1, str2, str3, sep = " ", collapse
= "")
```

14. Strings

```
#Concatenate using hiphen
concat2 = paste(str1, str2, str3, sep = "-", collapse
= "")
#Concatenate without any character
concat3 = paste(str1, str2, str3, sep = "", collapse
= "")
#Display all strings
print("Concatenated Strings: ")
print (concat1)
print (concat2)
print (concat3)
print("Extracting a substring from the first
concatenated string (7 to 20): ")
#Extract Substring
subs = substring(concat1, 7, 20)
#Display substrings
print (subs)
```

Output:

```
F:\R>Rscript strcatsubs.r
[1] "Concatenated Strings: "
[1] "World is a beautiful place!!!"
[1] "World-is a-beautiful place!!!"
[1] "Worldis abeautiful place!!!"
[1] "Extracting a substring from the first concatenated string (7 to 20): "
[1] "is a beautiful"

F:\R>
```

14.4 Miscellaneous String Operations

There are many more built-in functions while help in string manipulations. Let us take a look at a few more functions which we can use.

14.4.1 String length

There is a function called ***nchar*** which counts the number of characters in a string and effectively gives us the length of the string. Syntax:

nchar (<string>)

14.4.2 Upper and Lower case

The built-in functions – *toupper* and *tolower* can be used to convert a string to upper case and to lower case respectively. General Syntax:

toupper (<string>)
tolower (<string>)

Following is an R script that makes demonstrates miscellaneous string operation:

```
#Miscellaneous String Operations
#Initialize a few strings

s1 = "We are in the strings chapter of this eBook."
s2 = "R eBook"
s3 = "United States of America"

#Display all strings
cat("\ns1 = ", s1, "\ns2 = ", s2, "\ns3 = ", s3)
#Find the length of s1
len_s1 = nchar (s1)
#Display the length of s1
cat("\n\nLength of s1: ", len_s1)
#Conver s2 and s3 to upper and lower case and display
directly
cat("\n\nLower case s2: ", tolower(s2), "\nUpper case
s3: ", toupper(s3), "\n\n")
```

Output:

```
F:\R>Rscript miscstr.r
s1 = We are in the strings chapter of this eBook.
s2 = R eBook
s3 = United States of America

Length of s1:  44

Lower case s2:  r ebook
Upper case s3:  UNITED STATES OF AMERICA

F:\R>
```

15. Factors

Factors are categorical data objects used to classify data. For example, if there is a table which stores personal information of people and has columns such as name, age and gender. Let us consider the gender column. If we somehow extract this column and turn it into a vector, all it will have is – "Male" and "Female", repeated over and over again. The important thing here are the distinct categories – "Male" and "Female". These categories are known as *levels*. In simplest terms, for understanding sake, if you try to factor a vector, the unique elements from that vector will be extracted as levels. In order to convert a vector to a factor, you can use the *factor ()* function. General Syntax:

<factor_variable> = factor (<vector>)

You can check if a variable is of factor type by using the function *is.factor ()*. General Syntax:

is.factor(<variable>)

This function will return *TRUE* if the given variable is a factor, will return *FALSE* otherwise.

Let us assume a vector that stores the educational qualifications of people, consider the educational qualifications be Graduate, Post Graduate or Doctorate; and write an R script to factor this vector:

```
#Factor Demo
#Create an occupation vector
occupation    =    c("Graduate",    "Post    Graduate",
"Graduate", "Graduate", "Doctorate", "Post Graduate",
"Doctorate", "Graduate")
#Display occupation vector
```

```
cat("\n\nOccupation Vector\n\n")
print (occupation)
#Check if this is a factor
cat("\nIs       occupation      a      Factor?       \n",
is.factor(occupation))
#Convert to factor
fact_occupation = factor (occupation)
#Display fact_occupation
cat("\n\nOccupation Factor: \n")
print(fact_occupation)
#Check if this is a factor
cat("\nIs     fact_occupation     a     Factor?     \n",
is.factor(fact_occupation))
```

Output:

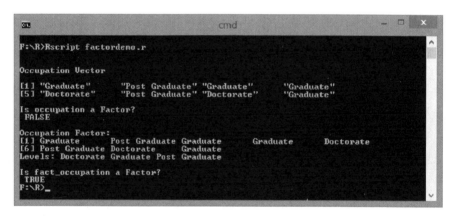

The usage and significance of factors will be clearer when we learn about **Data Frames** and **File Handling** in the chapters to follow.

16. Data Frames

A data frame is a two-dimensional data structure which is made up of rows and columns. For simplicity sake, we can think of a data frame as a table of data. This section is very important as it forms the basis for data handling in R. Hence, there are extensive programming examples in this section.

Consider the following table which stores personal information of different people:

id	name	age	country
1	Janice	23	USA
2	Tommy	31	Canada
3	Brad	25	Argentina

Here is a table having columns *id, name, age and country*. To store *id* and *age*, we need integer data types and to store *name* and *country*, we need string data types (character). As of now, there is a data of three people in this table. This example will be used to explain the concepts of this chapter.

If we want to create a data frame, we have to use the *data.frame()* function. A data frame is created using vectors. One column of data is one vector. In this example, we have 4 columns – *id, name, age and country*. To form a data frame, we will need four vectors, each for *id, name, age and country*. The general syntax of creating a data frame using the *data.frame ()* function is as follows:

data.frame (<column vector 1>, <column vector 2>, ... <column vector n>)

Example:
#Considering id, name, age and country are vectors
data_frame_1 = data.frame(id, name, age, country)

Refer to the following snippet where we create vectors for each of the columns of this table and form a data frame using the ***data.frame ()*** function:

```
#Data Frame Creation
#Vector for id column, fill 1 to 3
id <- c(1:3)
#Vector for name column
name <- c("Janice", "Tommy", "Brad")
#Vector for age column
age <- c(23, 31, 25)
#Vector for country column
country <- c("USA", "Canada", "Argentina")
#Create a data frame called person_df
person_df <- data.frame (id, name, age, country)
#Display the data frame
print (person_df)
```

Output:

```
F:\R>Rscript data_frame_creation.r
  id  name age   country
1  1 Janice  23       USA
2  2  Tommy  31    Canada
3  3   Brad  25 Argentina
F:\R>_
```

Take a look at the table we have at the start of this chapter and then take a look at this output. We have created the exact replica of the table programmatically using data frames.

16. Data Frames

A data frame can be created by forming vectors for each column while calling the ***data.frame ()*** function also. Here is how you would do it:

$Df\_1 = data.frame\ (<vector\ 1> = <vec\ 1\ values>, ... <vector\ n> = <vec\ n\ values>)$

Using this method to create the data frame of our table, our code would look like:

```
#Data Frame Creation 2
person_df <- data.frame ( id = c(1:3), name =
c("Janice", "Tommy", "Brad"), age = c(23, 31, 25))
print (person_df)
```

Output:

```
F:\R>Rscript data_frame_creation_2.r
  id  name age
1  1 Janice  23
2  2  Tommy  31
3  3   Brad  25

F:\R>
```

Notes:

1. All the columns within a data frame should be of the exact same length. If any of the columns do not have the same number of items, it will cause an error. Let us modify the first code from this section, give only two values for the country column instead of 3. Here is how the modified code would look like:

```
#Data Frame Creation Error Demo
#Vector for id column, fill 1 to 3
id <- c(1:3)
#Vector for name column
name <- c("Janice", "Tommy", "Brad")
```

```
#Vector for age column
age <- c(23, 31, 25)
#Vector for country column
#We are setting 2 values instead of 3
#This is wrong, only for demonstration purpose
country <- c("USA", "Canada")
#Create a data frame called person_df
person_df <- data.frame (id, name, age, country)
#Display the data frame
print (person_df)
```

Output:

```
F:\R>Rscript data_frame_creation.r
Error in data.frame(id, name, age, country) :
  arguments imply differing number of rows: 3, 2
Execution halted

F:\R>
```

The error gives you an idea of what is wrong with this code.

2. The variable names of the vector variables automatically become column names.

3. If you want to give custom names to columns, you can do so by creating a vector of column names and set it as follows:

   names (<data frame>) = <vector of column names>

   If we want to set the names of the columns to **person_id, person_name, person_age and person_country** instead of *id, name, age and country* after creating the data frame using *id, name, age and country vector variables*, we would use the following code:

   names (person_df) = c ("person_id", "person_name", "person_age", "person_country")

The column names should be non-empty when using custom names.

16.1 Accessing Data from Data Frames

When accessing data from data frames, it is possible to access rows, columns and individual elements. We will be looking at all these possibilities.

16.1.1 Accessing Rows

An entire row (with all columns) can be accessed using the following syntax:

<data frame>[<row number>,]

In our example, if we want to fetch the first row:

row_1 = *person_df [1,]*

This will return the first row as a list of values and hence there should be a variable to receive it unless you are trying to display the row directly.

Selective rows can be accessed in different ways. If rows from 3 to 6 need to be accessed, it can be does as follows:

<data frame>[3:6,]

If only second and fifth row need to be accessed, it can be done as follows:

<data frame>[c(2, 5),]

For all rows and all columns, use the following syntax:

<data frame> [,]

In our table example, we would use the following for all rows and columns:

person_df [,]

16.1.2 Accessing Columns

Columns of a data frame can be accessed using column names or column numbers. A column can be accessed using its name with the help of the following syntax:

<data frame>$<column name>

This will return the column as specified by the **<column name>** as a vector or a factor (explained in the next section) and hence there should be a variable to receive the returned vector or factor unless you want to display the column directly. In our table example, we would fetch each of the columns of the data frame as follows:

```
#id column
id = person_df$id
#name column
name = person_df$name
#age column
age = person_df$age
#country column
country = person_df$country
```

Columns can be accessed using numbers as follows:

For the entire column of all rows:

16. Data Frames

<data frame>[, <column number>]

Selective columns can be accessed in different ways. For columns from column numbers 2 to 5, use the following syntax:

<data frame>[, 2:5]

For columns with column number 1, 3, and 6, use the following syntax:

<data frame>[, c(1, 3, 6)]

For second and fourth column of third row, use the following syntax:

<data frame>[3, c(2, 4)]

Note: We have seen that vector names automatically become column names when we create a data frame. If you have renamed column names using **names(<data frame>)** function and are trying to access columns using column names, the new names should be used for this purpose. If you try to use the old name, no data will be fetched as that particular column name will no longer exist once it is replaced with the new name.

16.1.3 Accessing Individual Elements

Every element in a data frame has a corresponding row number and a column number. A particular element can be fetched with the following syntax:

<data frame>[<row number>, <column number>]

In our table example, we would use the following code to access individual elements:

#Element at first row, first column
elem1 = person_df [1, 1]

16.2 Factors in Data Frames

When a data frame is created with a vector column of string data, that column is automatically taken as a factor. To check this, we will modify the first code from this chapter to extract columns from the data frame and check if the columns are factors using *is.factor* function.

```
#Data Frame and Vectors
#Vector for id column, fill 1 to 3
id <- c(1:3)
#Vector for name column
name <- c("Janice", "Tommy", "Brad")
#Vector for age column
age <- c(23, 31, 25)
#Vector for country column
country <- c("USA", "Canada", "Argentina")
#Create a data frame called person_df
person_df <- data.frame (id, name, age, country)
#Display the data frame
print (person_df)
#Fetch all columns
column_id = person_df$id
column_name = person_df$name
column_age = person_df$age
column_country = person_df$country
#Display all columns and whether they are vectors or factors
#column_id
cat("\ncolumn_id column\n")
print (column_id)
cat ("\nIs factor? ", is.factor(column_id), "\nIs vector? " , is.vector(column_id))
#column_name
cat("\n\ncolumn_name column\n")
```

```
print (column_name)
cat ("\nIs factor? ", is.factor(column_name), "\nIs
vector? " , is.vector(column_name))
#column_age
cat("\n\ncolumn_age column\n")
print (column_age)
cat ("\nIs factor? ", is.factor(column_age), "\nIs
vector? " , is.vector(column_age))
#column_country
cat("\n\ncolumn_country column\n")
print (column_country)
cat ("\nIs factor? ", is.factor(column_country),
"\nIs vector? " , is.vector(column_country))
```

Output:

```
F:\R>Rscript data_frame_vectors.r
  id  name age   country
1  1 Janice  23       USA
2  2  Tommy  31    Canada
3  3   Brad  25 Argentina

column_id column
[1] 1 2 3

Is factor? FALSE
Is vector? TRUE

column_name column
[1] Janice Tommy  Brad
Levels: Brad Janice Tommy

Is factor? TRUE
Is vector? FALSE

column_age column
[1] 23 31 25

Is factor? FALSE
Is vector? TRUE

column_country column
[1] USA       Canada    Argentina
Levels: Argentina Canada USA

Is factor? TRUE
Is vector? FALSE
F:\R>
```

We have seen in the previous chapter that factors are categorical objects used to classify data into categories. When a data frame is created with atomic vectors of string (character) type, those vectors are automatically converted to factors. This auto-conversion is not an ideal thing is most situations. For example, if we had a column to store the gender of a person, auto-conversion of that column to a factor would have been fine as we could use gender to classify the records of that data frame. At the same time, a column that stores names in string (character) format would also be converted to a factor. This is not ideal for sure. Nobody wants to classify people based on their names. Think about it – you could use "male" and "female" to classify people. Sounds fine so far. How would it sound when you classify people having the name "David" into one category, "Jonathan" into another category, and so on. From a non-programmer's perspective, this situation would sound funny to say the least, but as a developer, this presents a problem and needs to be dealt with. Take a look at the previous output screengrab. The columns *name* and *country* are taken as factors. You could argue that *country* column can be considered as a factor but not *name* for sure. To counter auto-conversion of a column to a factor, there is a way out. While creating the data frame, you need to set the option ***stringsAsFactors*** to ***FALSE***. General Syntax:

data.frame (<column vector 1>, ..., stringsAsFactors = FALSE)

In our example, we would use the following line of code:

person_df <- data.frame (id, name, age, country, stringsAsFactors = FALSE)

Now, the output looks like this:

```
F:\R>Rscript data_frame_vectors.r
  id    name age   country
1  1  Janice  23       USA
2  2   Tommy  31    Canada
3  3    Brad  25 Argentina

column_id column
[1] 1 2 3

Is factor? FALSE
Is vector? TRUE

column_name column
[1] "Janice" "Tommy"  "Brad"

Is factor? FALSE
Is vector? TRUE

column_age column
[1] 23 31 25

Is factor? FALSE
Is vector? TRUE

column_country column
[1] "USA"     "Canada"  "Argentina"

Is factor? FALSE
Is vector? TRUE
F:\R>
```

16.3 Structure and Summary

The structure and the summary of a data frame can be retrieved using the *str(<data frame>)* and *summary(<data frame>)* functions respectively.

The code below shows the usage of these two functions:

```
#Structure and Summary
person_df <- data.frame ( id = c(1:3), name =
c("Janice", "Tommy", "Brad"), age = c(23, 31, 25),
country = c("USA", "Canada", "Argentina"),
stringsAsFactors = FALSE)
print (person_df)
cat("\n\nStrucure: \n\n")
print (str(person_df))
cat("\n\nSummary: \n\n")
print (summary(person_df))
```

Here is what our data frame's structure and summary looks like:

```
F:\R>Rscript dfstructuresummary.r
  id   name age   country
1  1 Janice  23       USA
2  2  Tommy  31    Canada
3  3   Brad  25 Argentina

Strucure:
'data.frame':   3 obs. of  4 variables:
 $ id      : int  1 2 3
 $ name    : chr  "Janice" "Tommy" "Brad"
 $ age     : num  23 31 25
 $ country : chr  "USA" "Canada" "Argentina"
NULL

Summary:
       id          name               age         country
 Min.   :1.0   Length:3         Min.   :23.00   Length:3
 1st Qu.:1.5   Class :character 1st Qu.:24.00   Class :character
 Median :2.0   Mode  :character Median :25.00   Mode  :character
 Mean   :2.0                    Mean   :26.33
 3rd Qu.:2.5                    3rd Qu.:28.00
 Max.   :3.0                    Max.   :31.00

F:\R>_
```

16.4 Data Frame Modification

We have seen how to access individual elements of a data frame using row and column number. With the same method, we could also change an element at a location. The general syntax for changing an element at a location is:

<data frame>[<row>, <column>] = <new value>

In our table example, value at location *[3,2]* is **"Brad"**. If we want to change it to something else, we would write the following code:

person_df [3, 2] = "Mike"

16.4.1 Adding a column

A new column can be added to an existing data frame by creating a new column vector first and then adding to the data frame using the following syntax:

16. Data Frames

<new column vector> = <vector elements>
<data frame>$<new column name> = <new column vector>

In our example, let us assume that we want to add another column called occupation. Consider that we want to add the following data shown in the new column (shown in green font):

id	name	age	country	occupation
1	Janice	23	USA	"Senior Developer"
2	Tommy	31	Canada	"Hedge fund Manager"
3	Brad	25	Argentina	"DevOps Engineer"

We would first form the occupation column vector as follows:

occupation = c("Senior Developer", "Hedge fund Manager", "DevOps Engineer")

Then, add this vector to the existing data frame as follows:

person_df$occupation = occupation

Here is the complete code:

```
#Data Frame Add Column
person_df <- data.frame ( id = c(1:3), name = c("Janice", "Tommy", "Brad"), age = c(23, 31, 25), country = c("USA", "Canada", "Argentina"), stringsAsFactors = FALSE)
print (person_df)
#Create occupation vector
occupation <- c("Senior Developer", "Hedge fund Manager", "DevOps Engineer")
#Add occupation vector to the existing data frame
person_df$occupation = occupation
cat("\n\nNew data frame:\n\n")
print (person_df)
```

Output:

```
F:\R>Rscript df_add_column.r
  id   name age   country
1  1 Janice  23       USA
2  2  Tommy  31    Canada
3  3   Brad  25 Argentina

New data frame:
  id   name age   country          occupation
1  1 Janice  23       USA    Senior Developer
2  2  Tommy  31    Canada Hedge fund Manager
3  3   Brad  25 Argentina     DevOps Engineer
F:\R>
```

16.4.2 Adding a row

When we add a row to a data frame, we are essentially adding a new record to the table-like data structure. In *Section 16.1.1*, we learned that when we extract a row from a data frame, it is returned as a *list*. If we want to add a new row, there are two methods — create a list of all values corresponding to each column of the new record and then add that list to the existing data structure or create a new data frame with the new records and bind the two data frames.

16.4.2.1 List as a Row

A list should be created first and then added to the data frame as follows:

<list variable> = list(<list elements>)
<data frame>[<row number>,] = <list variable>
Example:
list_1 = list (4, "Roger", 40, "Austria")
person_df [4,] = list_1

16. Data Frames

Let us recall the table from the beginning of *Chapter 16* and write code to insert the new row highlighted in yellow.

id	name	age	country
1	Janice	23	USA
2	Tommy	31	Canada
3	Brad	25	Argentina
4	Anita	29	UK

```
#Add Row As List
person_df <- data.frame ( id = c(1:3), name =
c("Janice", "Tommy", "Brad"), age = c(23, 31, 25),
country = c("USA", "Canada", "Argentina"),
stringsAsFactors = FALSE)
print (person_df)
#Create new list
new_row = list(4, "Anita", 29, "UK")
#Insert the 4th row
person_df[4, ] = new_row
cat("\n\nUpdated Data Frame\n")
print(person_df)
```

Output:

```
F:\>cd R
F:\R>Rscript df_list_as_row.r
  id  name age  country
1  1 Janice  23      USA
2  2  Tommy  31   Canada
3  3   Brad  25 Argentina

Updated Data Frame
  id  name age  country
1  1 Janice  23      USA
2  2  Tommy  31   Canada
3  3   Brad  25 Argentina
4  4  Anita  29       UK
F:\R>
```

16.4.2.2 Bind Data Frames

This is another method of adding rows to an existing data frame. The idea is simple; you create a new data frame with the exact same structure as the first data frame. Add data to the new data frame and bind the two data frames using ***rbind()*** function. General Syntax:

<new data frame> = rbind (<data frame 1>, <data frame 2>)
Example:
#Consider df1 and df2 are two data frames
df3 = rbind (df1, df2)

Let us recall the table from the beginning of ***Chapter 16*** and write code to insert the new rows highlighted in yellow.

id	name	age	country
1	Janice	23	USA
2	Tommy	31	Canada
3	Brad	25	Argentina
4	Anita	29	UK
5	Kane	43	Australia
6	Bella	32	Ireland

Here is the complete R script which creates two data frames and binds them together into a bigger data frame:

```
#Rbind Demo
#Create a data frame
person_df_1 <- data.frame ( id = c(1:3), name =
c("Janice", "Tommy", "Brad"), age = c(23, 31, 25),
```

16. Data Frames

```
    country = c("USA", "Canada", "Argentina"),
    stringsAsFactors = FALSE)
cat("\n\nperson_df_1 data frame:\n\n")
print (person_df_1)
#Create new data frame
person_df_2 <- data.frame ( id = c(4:6), name =
    c("Anita", "Kane", "Bella"), age = c(29, 43, 32),
    country = c("UK", "Australia", "Ireland"),
    stringsAsFactors = FALSE)
cat("\n\nperson_df_2 data frame:\n\n")
print(person_df_2)
#Bind person_df_1 and person_df_2
new_df <- rbind(person_df_1, person_df_2)
cat("\n\nNew data frame:\n\n")
print(new_df)
```

Output:

```
F:\R>Rscript df_rbind.r

person_df_1 data frame:

  id    name age   country
1  1  Janice  23       USA
2  2   Tommy  31    Canada
3  3    Brad  25 Argentina

person_df_2 data frame:

  id  name age   country
1  4 Anita  29        UK
2  5  Kane  43 Australia
3  6 Bella  32   Ireland

New data frame:

  id    name age   country
1  1  Janice  23       USA
2  2   Tommy  31    Canada
3  3    Brad  25 Argentina
4  4   Anita  29        UK
5  5    Kane  43 Australia
6  6   Bella  32   Ireland

F:\R>
```

Notes:

1. The number of elements in the list should be the same as the number of columns in the data frame.

2. The elements in the list should follow the same order as the columns in the data frame.

3. It is very important to set *stringsAsFactors* to *FALSE* because without it being set to *FALSE*, columns containing string data will be considered as factors, data from that column will be considered as levels and when you try to insert a new row with new data in one of the columns of string type which did not exist previously, the data frame will look at it as an invalid level thereby rejecting that particular column data and NA will be inserted instead.

16.5 Conditional Access of Data Frame Records

Data can be retrieved from a data frame by testing for one or more conditions. For example, from the previous table, if we want to retrieve only those records where age is less than 30 or retrieve only those records where country is USA, we can do so using the function called *subset( )*. This function fetches a subset of the given data frame by testing for a given condition. General Syntax:

<records data frame> = subset (<data frame>, <condition>)

Consider the following:

id	name	age	country	occupation
1	Janice	23	USA	"Senior Developer"
2	Tommy	31	Canada	"Hedge fund Manager"
3	Brad	25	Argentina	"DevOps Engineer"
4	Anita	29	UK	"Senior Developer"
5	Kane	43	Australia	"DevOps Engineer"
6	Bella	32	Ireland	"Accountant"

If you want to access record with *age* less than *30*, you would use the subset function in the following way:

records = subset (person_df, age < 30)

If you want to access records where *occupation* is *DevOps Engineer*, you would use the subset function in the following way:

records = subset (person_df, occupation == "DevOps Engineer")

If you want to fetch records where age is greater than 25 and occupation is Senior Developer, you would specify two conditions with Boolean AND operator as follows:

records = subset (person_df, age > 25 & occupation == "Senior Developer")

The *subset( )* function facilitates database-like access to some extent. Let us write an R script to demonstrate these concepts:

```
#Create a data frame
person_df <- data.frame ( id = c(1:6),
                          name = c("Janice",
"Tommy", "Brad", "Anita", "Kane", "Bella"),
    age = c(23, 31, 25, 29, 43, 32),
                          country = c("USA",
"Canada", "Argentina", "UK", "Australia", "Ireland"),
    occupation = c("Senior Developer", "Hedge fund
Manager", "DevOps Engineer", "Senior Developer",
"DevOps Engineer", "Accountant"),
    stringsAsFactors = FALSE)
cat("\n\nData Frame:\n\n")
print (person_df)
#Fetch records where age > 30
cat("\n\nRecords where age > 30\n")
records_1 <- subset(person_df, age > 30)
print(records_1)
#Fetch records where country == USA or UK
cat("\n\nRecords where country is USA or UK\n")
```

```r
records_2 <- subset(person_df, (country == "USA" |
country == "UK"))
print(records_2)
#Fetch records where occupation == "DevOps Engineer"
and age < 40
cat("\n\nRecords where occupation == DevOps Engineer
and age < 40 \n")
records_3 <- subset(person_df, (occupation == "DevOps
Engineer" & age < 30))
print(records_3)
```

Output:

```
F:\R>Rscript df_conditional_access.r

Data Frame:
  id   name age   country     occupation
1  1  Janice  23      USA    Senior Developer
2  2   Tommy  31   Canada    Hedge fund Manager
3  3    Brad  25 Argentina   DevOps Engineer
4  4   Anita  29       UK    Senior Developer
5  5    Kane  43 Australia   DevOps Engineer
6  6   Bella  32   Ireland   Accountant

Records where age > 30
  id   name age   country     occupation
2  2  Tommy   31   Canada    Hedge fund Manager
5  5   Kane   43 Australia   DevOps Engineer
6  6  Bella   32   Ireland   Accountant

Records where country is USA or UK
  id   name age country    occupation
1  1  Janice  23     USA  Senior Developer
4  4   Anita  29      UK  Senior Developer

Records where occupation == DevOps Engineer and age < 40
  id name age   country    occupation
3  3 Brad  25 Argentina DevOps Engineer

F:\R>
```

16.6 Access Data Frames with Loops

In this section, we will see how to access the elements of a data frame using loops. This method is not the best way, we have already seen simplified and better ways of accessing rows, columns and individual elements. However, we are studying this method because it offers a greater amount of control and is the most grass root level method. In order to use a loop, you should know how many

16. Data Frames

iterations to make. For that, you should know how many rows and columns are present in a data frame. The functions – *nrow (<data frame>)* and *ncol(<data frame>)* fetch the number of row and columns respectively in a given data frame.

We will be using two while loops in a nested manner, outer loop will keep track of the rows and the inner loop will keep track of the columns. We will be working with the same table present at the beginning of *Chapter 16*.

Here is the R script:

```r
#Data Frame and Loops
#Vector for id column, fill 1 to 3
id <- c(1:3)
#Vector for name column
name <- c("Janice", "Tommy", "Brad")
#Vector for age column
age <- c(23, 31, 25)
#Vector for country column
country <- c("USA", "Canada", "Argentina")
#Create a data frame called person_df
person_df <- data.frame (id, name, age, country, stringsAsFactors = FALSE)
#Find how many rows and columns
columns = ncol(person_df)
rows = nrow(person_df)
#Display the data frame using loops
#Inintialize two loop variables
count_row = 1
count_column = 1
cat("\n\nRows: ", rows, "Columns: ", columns)
#Iterate from 1 to rows
while (count_row <= rows) {
    cat("\n\nRow Number: ", count_row, "| Elements: \n\n")
    #Iterate form 1 to columns
    count_column = 1
    while(count_column <= columns) {
         #Display individual element
```

```
            cat(person_df[count_row, count_column], "  ")
            #Increment count_column
            count_column = count_column + 1
    }
    #Increment count_row
    count_row = count_row + 1
}
cat("\n\n")
```

Output:

```
F:\R>Rscript df_while_loop.r

Rows:  3 Columns:  4
Row Number:  1 | Elements:
1   Janice   23   USA
Row Number:  2 | Elements:
2   Tommy   31   Canada
Row Number:  3 | Elements:
3   Brad   25   Argentina

F:\R>
```

The data frames chapter is very important when it comes to dealing with data. The concepts learned here will be very helpful when working with data interfaces.

17. Basic File Handling

In this section we will learn the basics of accessing files on the system. The concepts learnt in this section will serve as a foundation for the next chapter which deals with Data Interfaces.

There are built in functions to work with files and directories. Let us look at the important ones.

Note: File handling on Windows is different from that of Linux and MAC. Necessary care needs to be taken when specifying file paths on different operating systems. Also, necessary permissions to the files and directories you want to work on are needed. Without that, you will run into errors.

17.1 Current Working Directory

Current working directory is the directory where the current R workspace is pointing to. In *Chapter 9*, we saw that while quitting the R Terminal, an option is given to the user of saving the Workspace. If the user opts to save the workspace, it will be saved in the current working directory. Similarly, any files that are created without giving the full path, they will be placed inside the current working directory. The function which is used to fetch the current working directory is – *getwd()*. This function returns the exact path of the current working directory in character form (string). It is possible to change the current working directory using the function – *setwd()*. General Syntax:

> *setcwd (<Directory Path>)*
> *Eg:*
> *#In Windows*
> *setcwd("F:/R")*

###OR###
setwd("F:\\R")
#In Linux/MAC
setwd ("/home/Chad/R")

Note: In most applications, Windows file paths are specified with a **backslash** *(\)*. In R, this character is used as an escape character. Hence, if you want to specify file path in Windows with a **backslash**, two **backslashes** *(\\)* should be used. For example, *D:\Tutorials\R_Scripts* will become *D:\\Tutorials\\R_Scripts*. Alternatively, you can use a single **forward slash** *(/)* like this – *D:/Tutorials/R_Scripts*.

Here is an R script that demonstrates the usage of **getwd** and **setwd** functions:

```
#Working Directory Demo
#Fetch working directory, store in a variable
working_directory <- getwd()
#Display working directory
cat("\nCurrent working directory: ", working_directory)
#Set working directory to C:/
cat("\nSet working directory to C:/")
setwd("C:/")
#Fetch new working directory
new_working_directory <- getwd()
#Display new working directory
cat("\nNew working directory - ", new_working_directory )
```

Output:

```
F:\R>Rscript wd_demo.r
Current working directory:  F:/R
Set working directory to C:/
New working directory -  C:/
F:\R>_
```

17.2 Working with files and directories

Here are a few important functions that help us in working with files and directories.

17.2.1 List all files in a directory

The function *list.files* is used to list all the files in a directory. General Syntax:

list.files(<Path to Directory>)

This function returns the names of all files present in the specified directory in character format. If no directory is specified, files from the working directory will be returned.

17.2.2 List subdirectories in a directory

The function *list.dirs* is used to list all the subdirectories in a directory. General Syntax:

list.dirs(<Path to Directory>)

This function returns the names of the directories present in the specified directory in character format. If no directory is specified, directories from the working directory will be returned.

17.2.3 Check if a file exists

You can check whether a file exists on the system with *file.exists* function. General Syntax:

file.exists(<Path to File>)

The ***file.exists*** function will return TRUE if the specified file exists else return false.

17.2.4 Create a file

The function ***file.create*** is used to create a new file. General Syntax:

file.create(<File Name>)

The file will be created in the working directory. If you want to create a file at a custom location, the working directory should be changed to the desired location first and then the file should be created using ***file.create*** function.

17.2.5 Remove a file

A file can be deleted using the ***file.remove*** function. General Syntax:

file.remove(<File Name>)

This function can also be used to delete directories on Unix based OS – Linux and MAC. This is because, everything in Unix is a file.

17.2.6 Rename a file

An existing file can be renamed using file.rename function. General Syntax:

file.rename(<Existing Name>, <New Name>)

17.2.7 Temporary file and directory

You can retrieve the location of temporary file and temporary directory on the system using the functions – *tempfile()* and *tempdir()* respectively.

Here is an R script that makes use of some of these functions:

```
#File Handling Demo
#Fetch working directory
working_directory <- getwd()
#Display working directory
cat("\nCurrent           working           directory:          ",
working_directory)
#Set working directory to F:/Codes
cat("\nSet working directory to F:/Codes")
setwd("F:/Codes")
#Fetch working directory
new_working_directory <- getwd()
#Display new working directory
cat("\nNew              working           directory:          ",
new_working_directory )
#Display all file names
cat("\nAll Files: \n")
print(list.files())
#Display all directory names
cat("\nAll Directories: \n")
print(list.dirs())
#Check if ecc.h exists
cat("\nCheck if ecc.h exists: \n")
print(file.exists("ecc.h"))
#Check if xyz.c exists
cat("\nCheck if xyz.c exists: \n")
print(file.exists("xyz.c"))
#Create a file
cat("\nCreating abc.txt\n")
file.create("abc.txt")
#Remove a file
cat("\nRemoving ecc.c\n")
file.remove("ecc.c")
#Display all files
cat("\nAll Files: \n")
print(list.files())
```

R Programming for Beginners

Output:

```
F:\R>Rscript filesdemo.r

Current working directory:  F:/R
Set working directory to F:/Codes
New working directory:  F:/Codes
All Files:
 [1] "address_generation_dump.txt" "C"
 [3] "C++"                          "ecc.c"
 [5] "ecc.h"                        "Java"
 [7] "Python"                       "R"
 [9] "screenshot1.png"              "test.txt"
[11] "testrequest.py"

All Directories:
[1] "."         "./C"       "./C++"     "./Java"    "./Python"  "./R"

Check if ecc.h exists:
[1] TRUE

Check if xyz.c exists:
[1] FALSE

Creating abc.txt
[1] TRUE

Removing ecc.c
[1] TRUE

All Files:
 [1] "abc.txt"           "address_generation_dump.txt"
 [3] "C"                 "C++"
 [5] "ecc.h"             "Java"
 [7] "Python"            "R"
 [9] "screenshot1.png"   "test.txt"
[11] "testrequest.py"

F:\R>
```

18. Data Interfaces

R is one of the best scripting languages for data mining, data science, BigData and other data handling requirements. These data techniques read data from huge data dumps such as databases or data files and work on the retrieved data. In this chapter, we will learn how to work with data files, extract data from them, add data to them. For that, we will learn two data interfaces – *CSV Data Interface* and *Excel Data Interface*. Before proceeding, it is very important to have a clear cut understanding of data frames. If you are not confident with data frame concepts, it is a good idea to go through *Chapter 16* all over again and try a few programming examples. The knowledge of basic file handling is also needed which is covered in *Chapter 17*. One common problem you may encounter as a beginner over and over again is you may not be able to able to open the desired file programmatically. This happens because the working directory is set to something and the file you may be trying to open is somewhere else. The concept of working directory is explained in *Section 17.1*.

18.1 CSV Data Interface

CSV stands for coma separated values. CSV format is used to represent meaningful data such as tables where individual values are separated using commas, hence the name comma separated values. The comma character is the de-facto delimiter to separate values but other characters such as semi colon can also be used. A CSV file can be created using any spreadsheet software such as Microsoft Excel or OpenOffice Spreadsheet. If you know your way around, you can even create the file manually using a text editor. In this section, we will learn to read and write CSV files using R.

Consider the following table of student data. We will use it as an example throughout this chapter.

id	name	stream	country	marks
1	Alexa	IT	Cyprus	65.8
2	Harvey	Electrical	UK	93.6
3	Gabriela	Telecommunication	Brazil	78.4
4	Ying	IT	China	81.5
5	Steven	Mechanical	UK	97.3
6	Jessica	IT	USA	68.4
7	Lee	Electrical	China	59.4

Let us turn this into a CSV file using Microsoft Excel. This is what the spreadsheet would look like:

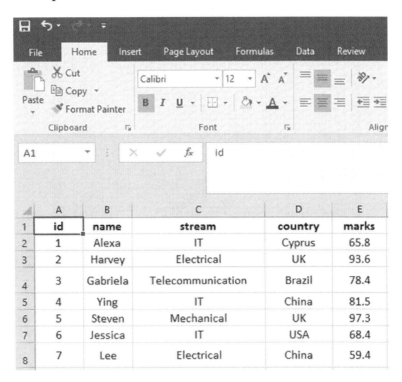

Now, we save this file as ***student_data.csv*** at a convenient location. Following is the plaintext contents of this CSV file when opened using a text editor:

```
id,name,stream,country,marks
1,Alexa,IT,Cyprus,65.8
2,Harvey,Electrical,UK,93.6
3,Gabriela,Telecommunication,Brazil,78.4
4,Ying,IT,China,81.5
5,Steven,Mechanical,UK,97.3
6,Jessica,IT,USA,68.4
7,Lee,Electrical,China,59.4
```

18.1.1 Reading CSV Files

A CSV file can be read using the ***read.csv( )*** function. This function reads the given CSV file, fetches the data and returns it as a ***Data Frame***. General Syntax:

<data frame variable> = read.csv(<csv file>)

If we want to read the previously created ***student_data.csv*** file, we would write code that would look like this:

student_df = read.csv ("student_data.csv")

Notes:

1. Make sure that the working directory has been set to a location where your CSV file is present.

2. Make sure you have the right permissions to the directory/file.

3. You can specify complete or relative path to the file.

Let us write a simple R script to read this CSV file and display the data frame.

```
#Basic CSV Read Demo
#Set Working Directory
#IMPORTANT: SET YOUR OWN DIRECTORY WHICH IS
ACCESSIBLE
setwd("F:/R/")
#Read CSV file, store in a data frame
student_df <- read.csv("student_data.csv")
#Display Data Frame
cat("\nCSV File Read as Data Frame:\n")
print (student_df)
#Display rows and columns
cat("\n\nRows:", nrow(student_df), "Columns:",
ncol(student_df), "\n")
#Check if data frame
cat("\nIs student_df a Data Frame? - ",
is.data.frame(student_df), "\n\n")
```

Output:

```
F:\R>Rscript csv_read.r
CSV File Read as Data Frame:
  id    name          stream country marks
1  1   Alexa              IT  Cyprus  65.8
2  2  Harvey      Electrical      UK  93.6
3  3 Gabriela Telecommunication Brazil 78.4
4  4    Ying              IT   China  81.5
5  5  Steven      Mechanical      UK  97.3
6  6 Jessica              IT     USA  68.4
7  7     Lee      Electrical   China  59.4

Rows: 7 Columns: 5
Is student_df a Data Frame? -  TRUE

F:\R>
```

Let us fetch all columns one by one and check if they are vectors or factors:

```
#Check column data types
#Set Working Directory
setwd("F:/R/")
#Read CSV file, store in a data frame
student_df <- read.csv("student_data.csv")
#Display Data Frame
cat("\nCSV File Read as Data Frame:\n")
print (student_df)
#Fetch all columns
```

18. Data Interfaces

```
id = student_df$id
name = student_df$name
stream = student_df$stream
country = student_df$country
marks = student_df$marks
#Display all columns and check if they are vectors or factors
cat("\nid:\n")
print(id)
cat("\nIs id vector? - ", is.vector(id), "| Is id factor? - ", is.factor(id), "\n")
cat("\nname: \n")
print(name)
cat("\nIs name vector? - ", is.vector(name), "| Is name factor? - ", is.factor(name), "\n")
cat("\nstream: \n")
print(stream)
cat("\nIs stream vector? - ", is.vector(stream), "| Is stream factor? - ", is.factor(stream), "\n")
cat("\ncountry: \n")
print(country)
cat("\nIs country vector? - ", is.vector(country), "| Is country factor? - ", is.factor(country), "\n")
cat("\nmarks:\n ")
print(marks)
cat("\nIs marks vector? - ", is.vector(marks), "| Is marks factor? - ", is.factor(marks), "\n\n")
```

Output:

```
F:\R>Rscript csv_read_columns.r
CSV File Read as Data Frame:
  id    name          stream    country  marks
1  1   Alexa              IT     Cyprus   65.8
2  2   Harvey      Electrical       UK    93.6
3  3  Gabriela Telecommunication  Brazil  78.4
4  4    Ying              IT      China   81.5
5  5   Steven      Mechanical       UK    97.3
6  6   Jessica            IT       USA    68.4
7  7    Lee        Electrical    China    59.4
id:
[1] 1 2 3 4 5 6 7
Is id vector? - TRUE ! Is id factor? - FALSE
name:
[1] Alexa    Harvey   Gabriela Ying    Steven  Jessica  Lee
Levels: Alexa Gabriela Harvey Jessica Lee Steven Ying
Is name vector? - FALSE ! Is name factor? - TRUE
stream:
[1] IT              Electrical     Telecommunication IT
[5] Mechanical      IT             Electrical
Levels: Electrical IT Mechanical Telecommunication
Is stream vector? - FALSE ! Is stream factor? - TRUE
country:
[1] Cyprus UK     Brazil China  UK     USA    China
Levels: Brazil China Cyprus UK USA
Is country vector? - FALSE ! Is country factor? - TRUE
marks:
[1] 65.8 93.6 78.4 81.5 97.3 68.4 59.4
Is marks vector? - TRUE ! Is marks factor? - FALSE
```

As seen from the output, columns with string data are taken as factors and not as vectors. This problem is similar to the one we learned in *Section 16.2*. Over there, we ran into this problem while creating the data frame manually and over here, we face the same problem when a CSV file is read as a data frame. The solution is the same. In *read.csv( )* function, you have to set *stringsAsFactors* to *FALSE* as follows:

<data frame variable> = read.csv(<csv file>, stringsAsFactors = FALSE)

If we want to read the previously created *student_data.csv* file with *stringsAsFactors* option set to *FALSE*, we would write code that would look like this:

18. Data Interfaces

student_df = read.csv ("student_data.csv", stringsAsFactors = FALSE)

With this change, our output would look like this:

```
F:\R>Rscript csv_read_columns.r
CSV File Read as Data Frame:
  id    name             stream country marks
1  1   Alexa                 IT  Cyprus  65.8
2  2  Harvey         Electrical      UK  93.6
3  3 Gabriela Telecommunication  Brazil  78.4
4  4    Ying                 IT   China  81.5
5  5  Steven         Mechanical      UK  97.3
6  6 Jessica                 IT     USA  68.4
7  7     Lee         Electrical   China  59.4
id:
[1] 1 2 3 4 5 6 7
Is id vector? - TRUE ! Is id factor? - FALSE
name:
[1] "Alexa"   "Harvey"  "Gabriela" "Ying"  "Steven"  "Jessica" "Lee"
Is name vector? - TRUE ! Is name factor? - FALSE
stream:
[1] "IT"              "Electrical"         "Telecommunication"
[4] "IT"              "Mechanical"         "IT"
[7] "Electrical"
Is stream vector? - TRUE ! Is stream factor? - FALSE
country:
[1] "Cyprus" "UK"    "Brazil" "China"  "UK"    "USA"    "China"
Is country vector? - TRUE ! Is country factor? - FALSE
marks:
[1] 65.8 93.6 78.4 81.5 97.3 68.4 59.4
Is marks vector? - TRUE ! Is marks factor? - FALSE
F:\R>
```

Now, all columns are taken as vectors.

Let us write another R script to read the same CSV file, fetch the data in a data frame and create another data frame which will contain records which have the stream field as *"IT"*. This has less to do with CSV files and more to do with data frames; to be precise, we learned about this concept in ***Section 16.5***. Here is the R script:

```
#CSV Read, conditional DF Access
#Set Working Directory
#IMPORTANT:   SET   YOUR   OWN   DIRECTORY   WHICH   IS
ACCESSIBLE
```

```
setwd("F:/R/")
#Read CSV file, store in a data frame
student_df <- read.csv("student_data.csv")
#Display Data Frame
cat("\nOriginal CSV File:\n")
print (student_df)
#Display rows and columns
cat("\n\nRows:",    nrow(student_df),    "Columns:",
ncol(student_df), "\n")
#Fetch records with stream == "IT"
student_it_df = subset (student_df, stream == "IT")
#Display Data Frame
cat("\nNew Data Frame where stream == IT:\n")
print (student_it_df)
#Display rows and columns
cat("\n\nRows:",    nrow(student_it_df),    "Columns:",
ncol(student_it_df), "\n")
```

Output:

```
F:\R>Rscript csv_conditions.r
Original CSV File:
  id    name          stream country marks
1  1   Alexa              IT  Cyprus  65.8
2  2  Harvey       Electrical     UK  93.6
3  3 Gabriela Telecommunication Brazil 78.4
4  4    Ying              IT   China  81.5
5  5  Steven       Mechanical     UK  97.3
6  6 Jessica              IT     USA  68.4
7  7     Lee       Electrical  China  59.4

Rows: 7 Columns: 5
New Data Frame where stream == IT:
  id    name stream country marks
1  1   Alexa     IT  Cyprus  65.8
4  4    Ying     IT   China  81.5
6  6 Jessica     IT     USA  68.4

Rows: 3 Columns: 5
F:\R>
```

18.1.2 Writing to CSV Files

In this section, we will see how to write data to CSV files. Just as when you read a CSV file, a data frame is returned, a data frame can be written to a CSV file and the resultant data will be converted to the appropriate CSV format. There is a function called ***write.csv( )*** which is used to write a data frame to a CSV file. General syntax:

write.csv(<data frame>, <output csv file>)

If you have a data frame called ***df*** and want to write its data to a file called ***output.csv*** file, this is what you would do:

write.csv(df, "output.csv")

It goes without saying that the output file will be created in the working directory unless the full path is specified.

Let us understand this concept with the help of an example. Consider the following table. We will create a data frame and write it to a CSV file.

company	model	engine_capacity (cc)
Audi	Q7	2967
BMW	528i	1999
Jaguar	XF	1998
Land Rover	Range Rover Velar	2993

Here is an R script that creates a data frame of this table and writes it to a CSV file called ***cars.csv***:

```
#Simple CSV Write Demo
#Create vectors for data frame
company <- c("Audi", "BMW", "Jaguar", "Land Rover")
model <- c("Q7", "528i", "XF", "Range Rover Velar")
engine_capacity <- c(2967, 1999, 1998, 2993)
#Create Data Frame
cars_df       <-      data.frame(company,     model,
engine_capacity, stringsAsFactors = FALSE)
#Display Data Frame
```

```
print(cars_df)
#Write this data frame to file cars.csv
write.csv(cars_df, "cars.csv")
cat("\n\nSuccessully written to file cars.csv\n\n")
```

Output:

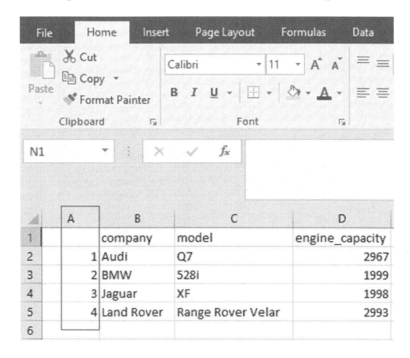

If you open *cars.csv* file, you will see something like this:

We got the data right for the most part, however and extra column (highlighted in red) is inserted. This is because, when you

18. Data Interfaces

create a data frame, every row is given a unique name which happens to be incremental serial numbers starting from 1 in case no names are specified. If you want to get rid of this, set the option *row.names* to *FALSE* when writing to the CSV file using the *write.csv* function as follows:

write.csv (<data frame>, <output csv>, row.names = FALSE)

When *row.names* is set to FALSE in the previous code, the CSV file looks like this:

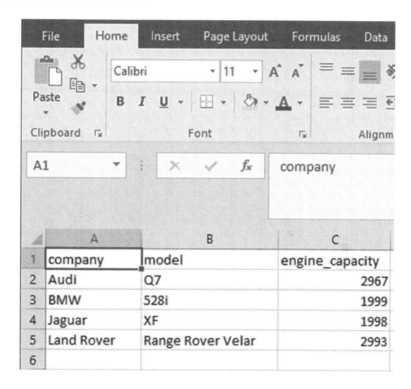

As seen, the auto generated first column is no longer present.

Let us work on an R script that combines reading and writing from and to CSV files. Recall the *student_data.csv* file from *Section 18.1* which looks like this:

	A	B	C	D	E
1	id	name	stream	country	marks
2	1	Alexa	IT	Cyprus	65.8
3	2	Harvey	Electrical	UK	93.6
4	3	Gabriela	Telecommunication	Brazil	78.4
5	4	Ying	IT	China	81.5
6	5	Steven	Mechanical	UK	97.3
7	6	Jessica	IT	USA	68.4
8	7	Lee	Electrical	China	59.4

We will read this CSV file, select records where **stream** is **IT** and put them in a new CSV file called **student_it.csv**, select records where **country** is **UK** and put them in another CSV file called **student_uk.csv**. Here is the complete R script:

```
#CSV Read and Write
#Set Working Directory
#IMPORTANT: SET YOUR OWN DIRECTORY WHICH IS
ACCESSIBLE
setwd("F:/R/")
#Read CSV file, store in a data frame
student_df <- read.csv("student_data.csv")
#Display Data Frame
cat("\nOriginal CSV File:\n")
print (student_df)
#Fetch records with stream == "IT"
student_it_df = subset (student_df, stream == "IT")
#Fetch records with country == "UK"
student_uk_df = subset (student_df, country == "UK")
#Display Data Frame
```

18. Data Interfaces

```
cat("\nIT Students\n")
print (student_it_df)
#Display Data Frame
cat("\nUK Students\n")
print (student_uk_df)
#Write student_it_df and student_uk_df to two
separate CSV files
write.csv(student_it_df, "student_it.csv", row.names
= FALSE)
write.csv(student_uk_df, "student_uk.csv", row.names
= FALSE)
cat("\n\nTwo new files created successfully.\n\n")
```

Output:

```
F:\R>Rscript csv_read_write.r
Original CSV File:
  id    name            stream   country  marks
1  1   Alexa                IT    Cyprus   65.8
2  2  Harvey         Electrical       UK   93.6
3  3 Gabriela Telecommunication    Brazil   78.4
4  4    Ying                IT     China   81.5
5  5  Steven        Mechanical        UK   97.3
6  6 Jessica                IT       USA   68.4
7  7     Lee        Electrical     China   59.4
IT Students
  id    name stream country marks
1  1   Alexa     IT  Cyprus  65.8
4  4    Ying     IT   China  81.5
6  6 Jessica     IT     USA  68.4
UK Students
  id    name     stream country marks
2  2  Harvey Electrical      UK  93.6
5  5  Steven Mechanical      UK  97.3

Two new files created successfully.

F:\R>
```

Let us open ***student_it.csv*** and ***student_uk.csv*** files separately and see what they look like.

Output (student_it.csv):

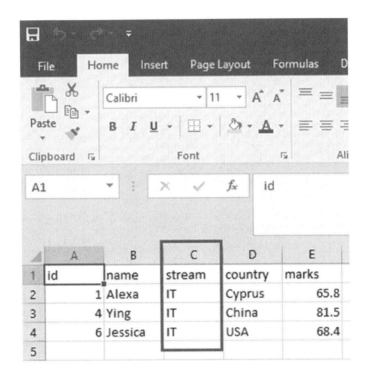

Output (student_uk.csv)

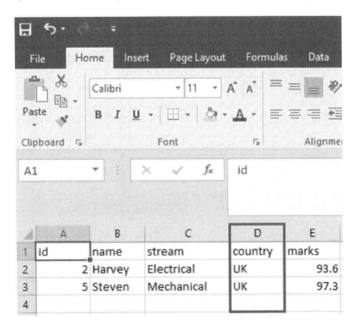

18.2 Excel Data Interface

Microsoft Excel is one of the most used spreadsheet software. While it supports various file formats, the default spreadsheet file types have the extensions *.xls* or *.xlsx*. Excel files *(.xls and .xlsx)* can be accessed from R using a package called *xlsx*. This package is not shipped with the default R distribution. You have to install it and you will need an internet connection to do so. To install *xlsx* package, open **Command Prompt** on Windows or **Terminal/Shell** on MAC/Linux and start the **R Terminal** by giving the **R** command. Inside the R Terminal, enter the following command:

install.packages("xlsx")

Follow the instructions, it may ask you to select a download mirror for downloading the relevant files. This may take a while. Once the installation process is complete, run the following command inside the R Terminal to check if the *xlsx* package has been installed successfully:

any(grepl("xlsx",installed.packages()))

This command should return **TRUE** as shown below:

Note: The ***xlsx*** package requires the latest stable Java Framework. Otherwise many warnings will be raised when you try to use this package.

Whenever you work with this package, it should be loaded into the workspace using the ***library()*** function as follows:

library ("xlsx")

If you are working with Excel files through the R Terminal, this statement should be entered before you try to read or write Excel files. Similarly, if you are writing an R script to work with Excel files, this statement should be present before the statements which try to access Excel files. It is a good idea to insert this statement at the beginning of the script.

Recall the table from ***Section 18.1.*** Let us put the same data into a spreadsheet and save it as ***student_data.xlsx.*** Here is a screengrab of the spreadsheet:

	A	B	C	D	E
1	id	name	stream	country	marks
2	1	Alexa	IT	Cyprus	65.8
3	2	Harvey	Electrical	UK	93.6
4	3	Gabriela	Telecommunication	Brazil	78.4
5	4	Ying	IT	China	81.5
6	5	Steven	Mechanical	UK	97.3
7	6	Jessica	IT	USA	68.4
8	7	Lee	Electrical	China	59.4

This demo spreadsheet will be used to explain the concepts of this section.

18.2.1 Reading Excel Files

An Excel file can be read using the ***read.xlsx()*** function. This function reads the given Excel file and returns the data as a ***Data Frame***. General Syntax:

<data frame variable> = read.xlsx(<Excel file>, sheetIndex = <index>)

If we want to read the previously created ***student_data.xlsx*** file, we would write code that would look like this:

student_df = read.xlsx ("student_data.xlsx", sheetIndex = 1)

Notes:

1. Make sure that the working directory has been set to a location where your Excel file is present.

2. Make sure you have the right permissions to the directory/file.

3. You can specify complete or relative path to the file.

4. If there are multiple sheets in your spreadsheet and you want to read a particular sheet, you can specify its index by setting ***sheetIndex***. For example, if you want to read the ***third*** sheer, you can set ***sheetIndex*** to *3* in the ***read.xlsx*** function.

Let us write a simple R script to read ***student_data.xlsx*** and display the data frame.

```
#Basic Excel Read Demo
#Load xlsx library into the workspace
library("xlsx")
#Set Working Directory
#IMPORTANT: SET YOUR OWN DIRECTORY WHICH IS ACCESSIBLE
setwd("F:/R/")
#Read Excel file, store in a data frame
student_df    <-    read.xlsx("student_data.xlsx", sheetIndex = 1)
#Display Data Frame
cat("\nExcel File Read as Data Frame:\n")
print (student_df)
#Display rows and columns
cat("\n\nRows:",   nrow(student_df),   "Columns:", ncol(student_df), "\n")
#Check if data frame
cat("\nIs   student_df   a   Data   Frame?   -   ", is.data.frame(student_df), "\n\n")
```

Output:

```
Excel File Read as Data Frame:
  id   name            stream         country  marks
1  1   Alexa                    IT    Cyprus   65.8
2  2   Harvey           Electrical        UK   93.6
3  3   Gabriela Telecommunication    Brazil   78.4
4  4   Ying                     IT     China   81.5
5  5   Steven           Mechanical        UK   97.3
6  6   Jessica                  IT       USA   68.4
7  7   Lee              Electrical    China   59.4

Rows: 7 Columns: 5
Is student_df a Data Frame?  -  TRUE

F:\R>
```

Note: By default, columns with string content will be taken as factors. To counter this, you can set ***stringsAsFactors*** to ***FALSE*** in the ***read.xlsx()*** function as follows:

<df variable> = read.xlsx(<Excel file>, sheetIndex = <index>, stringsAsFactors = FALSE)

18.2.2 Writing to Excel Files

In this section, we will see how to write data to Excel files. You can create a data frame and write it to an Excel File using the **write.xlsx()** function. General syntax:

write.xlsx(<data frame>, <Excel file>)

If you have a data frame called **df** and want to write its data to a file called **output.xlsx** file, this is what you would do:

write.xlsx(df, "output.xlsx")

By default, row names of the data frame will be inserted as a column in the spreadsheet. You can disable this by setting **row.names** to **FALSE** in the **write.xlsx** function like this:

write.xlsx(<data frame>, <Excel file>, row.names = FALSE)

Let us create the data frame of the following table and write it to an Excel spreadsheet.

make	model	chipset	ram	rom
Sony	Xperia 5	Snapdragon 855	6	128
Samsung	Galaxy A80	Snapdragon 730	8	128
HTC	Wildfire X	Helio P22	3	32

Here is the R script:

```
#Write to Excel Spreadsheer
#Load xlsx package
library("xlsx")
#Set Working Directory
setwd("F:/R/")
#Create vectors for data frame
make <- c("Sony", "Samsung", "HTC")
```

```
model <- c("Xperia 5", "Galaxy A80", "Wildfire X")
ram <- c(6, 8, 3)
rom <- c(128, 128, 32)
#create data frame
phone_df <- data.frame(make, model, ram, rom,
stringsAsFactors = FALSE)
#Display data frame
cat("\n\nPhone Data Frame:\n\n")
print(phone_df)
#Write to Excel Spreadsheet at index 1
write.xlsx(phone_df , "phone_data.xlsx", row.names =
FALSE )
cat("\n\nData    Frame    written    successfully    to
phone_data.xlsx\n")
```

Output:

```
F:\R>Rscript excel_write.r

Phone Data Frame:

       make      model ram rom
1      Sony   Xperia 5   6 128
2   Samsung Galaxy A80   8 128
3       HTC Wildfire X   3  32

Data Frame written successfully to phone_data.xlsx
F:\R>
```

Let us open the programmatically created *phone_data.xlsx* and see what it looks like:

18. Data Interfaces

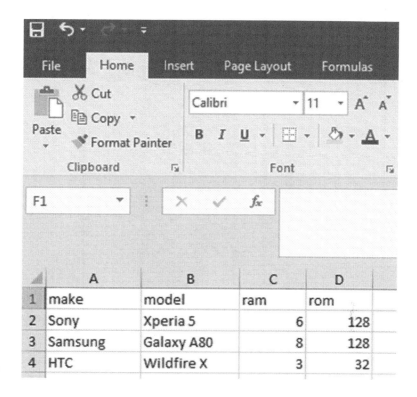

Turns out, the table has been exactly replicated first as a data frame and then written to an Excel sheet.

R's simplified way of working with CSV and Excel files makes it a very powerful tool for data analysis. If you are interested in this line of work professional or even as a hobbyist, I suggest you work with different data sets and establish a strong foundation in this field because the age of data is already here!

19. Data Visualization

R offers a rich set of tools for data visualization. We will be studying only the simple ones – pie chart, bar chart and line graph.

19.1 Pie Chart

A pie chart is a data visualization statistical graphic where a circle is divided into slices. The arc length of each size is proportional to the numeric value it represents. In R, a pie chart can be drawn using a function called *pie()*. General Syntax:

pie(<x>, <labels>, <radius>, <main>, <col>, <clockwise>)
Where:

<x> - Vector of numeric values, each value represents proportionate arc length of each pie slice.

<labels> - Vector of strings, each value represents the text label of each pie slice.

<radius> - Radius of the circle.

<main> - Title of the pie chart. Should be a string.

<col> - Colour pallet to be used. Vector of colour names.

<clockwise> - Start drawing clockwise or anticlockwise. Either TRUE or FALSE.

Out of all these arguments, only **<x>** and **<labels>** are the mandatory ones, rest are optional. The number of elements in **<x>** should be the same as the ones in **<labels>**.

This function when called from the R terminal will launch a window which will display the pie chart. Whereas, if this function is called through an R script, no GUI will launch and the pie chart will be lost. In order to retain that pie chart, it will have to be programmatically saved to an image file. We will see how to do that later in this section, let us now see how to draw a pie chart through the R terminal. Consider the following table with mock data:

text_lables	values
A	34
B	76
C	23
D	83
E	19

Open R terminal, create ***text_labels*** and ***values*** vectors as follows:

text_labels = c("A", "B", "C", "D", "E")

values = c(34,76,23,83,19)

Now call the pie function as follows:

pie(values, tex_labels)

This is what the R terminal will look like:

```
You are welcome to redistribute it under certain conditions.
Type 'license()' or 'licence()' for distribution details.

  Natural language support but running in an English locale

R is a collaborative project with many contributors.
Type 'contributors()' for more information and
'citation()' on how to cite R or R packages in publications.

Type 'demo()' for some demos, 'help()' for on-line help, or
'help.start()' for an HTML browser interface to help.
Type 'q()' to quit R.

> text_labels = c("A", "B", "C", "D", "E")
> values = c(34,76,23,83,19)
> pie(values, text_labels)
>
```

19. Data Visualization

When you call the pie function, you will notice that another window launches containing the pie chart:

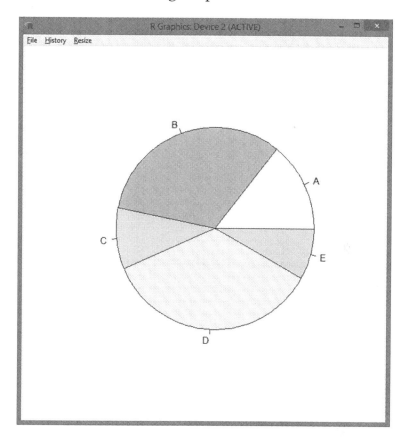

Through this window, you can manually save the file if you want from the *File -> Save as -> [FORMAT]* menu option.

Let us see how we can set the title and the colour pallet. The title of the chart can be set using the *main* argument and colour pallet can be used by setting the *col* argument. For example, *main = "Demo Pie Chart"* would set the title and the best way to set a colour pallet is to use the *rainbow(<number>)* function which returns a vector of colours. This function needs the number of colours to be used as an argument. In most cases, the number of colours to be used will be equal to the number of number of elements in *labels* or *x* vector. Alternatively, you can use a vector with colour names. For example: *col = c("red", "blue", "green")*. Making use of these concepts, this is how we will call the pie function now having made no changes to the *values* and *text_labels* vectors:

pie(values, text_labels, main = "Demo Pie Chart" , col = rainbow(length(values)))

You should see a pie chart like this:

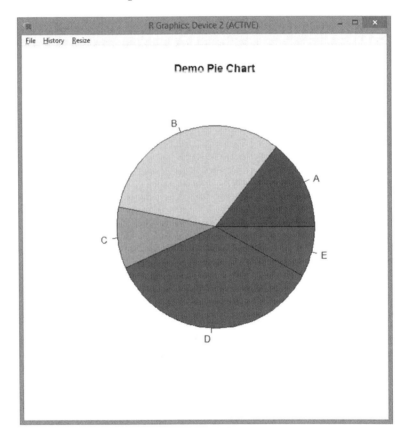

19. Data Visualization

Alternatively, you can form a vector of colour names as your colour pallet and then assign that vector to the col argument as shown below:

colour_pallet = c("cyan", "yellow", "red", "green", "orange")
pie(values, text_labels, main = "Demo Pie Chart" , col = colour_pallet)

You should see a pie chart like this:

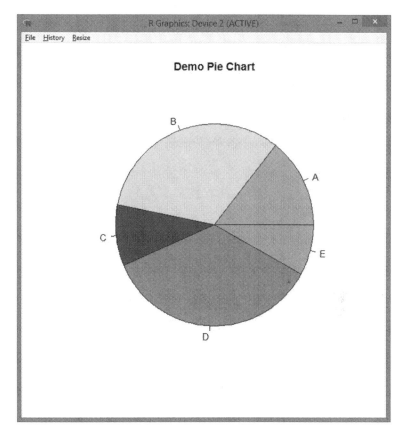

Now that we have seen how to draw a pie chart, let us understand how to write a script with this function in it and save the chart to a file. For this, you have to follow the below mentioned steps while writing the R script:

Step 1: Create the required vectors. Eg: x vector, labels vector, etc.

Step 2: Call the *png ( )* function to set the output file name as follows:

> *png (file = <output file name>)*
> *Example:*
> *png (file = "demo_pie_chart.png")*

Note: This file will be created in the working directory.

Step 3: Call the pie function.

Step 4: Call the *dev.off( )* function. This function closes the plotting device. The specifics of *dev.off( )* function requires the understanding of I/O concepts and is beyond the scope of this book. At an abstracted level, consider that the plotting device is the output file and this function save the file.

Combining all these concepts, let us write an R script to plot the pie chart of the data given in the table at the beginning of this chapter and save it to a file called *"demo_pie_chart.png"*.

```
#Pie Chart Demo
#Set working directory
#IMPORTANT: SET YOUR OWN DIRECTORY WHICH IS ACCESSIBLE
setwd("F:/R")
#Create requisite vectors for plotting pie chart
text_labels = c("A", "B", "C", "D", "E")
values = c(34,76,23,83,19)
#Set output image file name where the pie chart will be saved
png ( file = "demo_pie_chart.png")
#Call the pie function
```

19. Data Visualization

```
pie(values, text_labels, main = "Demo Pie Chart",
col = rainbow(length(values)))
#Close the plotting device. I.e. Save the output file
dev.off()
```

Run this R script:

You will notice that the output file *"demo_pie_chart.png"* is created inside the working directory. This is what it will look like:

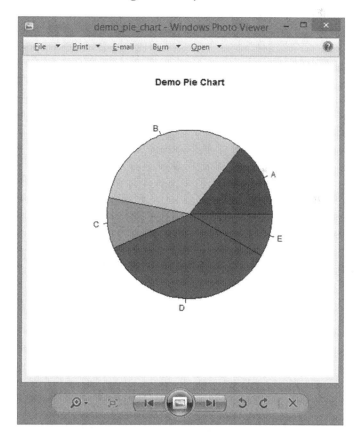

19.2 Bar Chart

A bar chart or a bar graph is a statistical graphic where in rectangular bars are used to represent numeric data. In R, a bar chart can be drawn using the ***barplot ()*** function. General Syntax:

barplot(<H>, <xlab> , <ylab> , <main> , <names.arg>, <col>)
Where:
<H> - Vector of numeric values to be plotted in the chart.
<xlab> - Label for x-axis
<ylab> - Label for y-axis
<main> - Title of the pie chart. Should be a string.
<names.arg> - Vector of labels for each bar.
<col> - Colour of the bars.

When you call this function through the R terminal, a window will pop-up which will contain the bar chart. If you want to write a script to plot a bar chart, you will have to save it to an image file. The procedure is similar to the one mentioned at the end of ***Section 19.1*** which explains how to create a pie chart using an R script; except, you need to call ***barplot()*** function instead of ***pie( )*** function in ***Step 2***.

Here is the monthly rainfall data of Hong Kong for the year 2018 provided by Hong Kong Observatory.

19. Data Visualization

Month	Rainfall (mm)
January	62.2
February	4.5
March	22.7
April	28.1
May	57.5
June	458.8
July	341.1
August	615.1
September	383.3
October	104.3
November	73.4
December	11.9

Let us plot the bar chart first using the R terminal and later using an R script. To begin with the R terminal, we need to create the vectors of month names and rainfall data. Here's how to do that:

rainfall <- c(62.2, 4.5, 22.7, 28.1, 57.5, 458.8, 341.1, 615.1, 383.3, 104.3, 73.4, 11.9)

month_names <- c("Jan", "Feb", "Mar", "Apr", "May", "Jun", "Jul", "Aug", "Sep", "Oct", "Nov", "Dec")

Call the bar plot function as follows:

barplot(rainfall, xlab = "Year 2018", ylab = "Rainfall (in mm)", main = "Rainfall data for Hong Kong (2018)", names.arg = month_names, col = "green")

A window will launch with the bar chart and will look something like this:

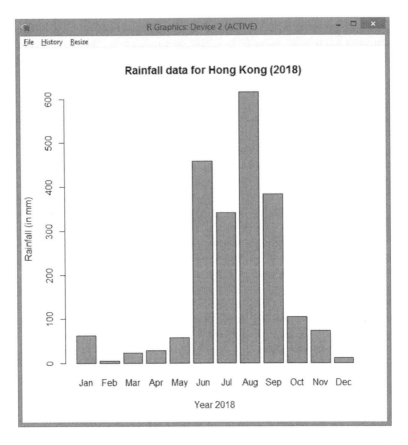

Having understood how to plot a bar chart through the R terminal, it is not time to write an R script to generate the bar chart programmatically and save it to an image file. We will name this file as *"rainfall_bar_chart.png"*, colour the bars in **cyan** and only use initials for month names.

```
#Bar Chart Demo
#Set working directory
#IMPORTANT: SET YOUR OWN DIRECTORY WHICH IS ACCESSIBLE
setwd("F:/R")
```

19. Data Visualization

```
#Create requisite vectors for plotting bar chart
rainfall <- c(62.2, 4.5, 22.7, 28.1, 57.5, 458.8,
341.1, 615.1, 383.3, 104.3, 73.4, 11.9)
#month_names <- c("Jan", "Feb", "Mar", "Apr", "May",
"Jun", "Jul", "Aug", "Sep", "Oct", "Nov", "Dec")
month_names <- c("J", "F", "M", "A", "M", "J", "J",
"A", "S", "O", "N", "D")
#Set output image file name where the bar chart will
be saved
png ( file = "rainfall_bar_chart.png")
#Call the bar plot function
barplot(rainfall, xlab = "Year 2018", ylab =
"Rainfall (in mm)", main = "Rainfall data for Hong
Kong (2018)", names.arg = month_names, col = "cyan")
#Close the plotting device. I.e. Save the output file
dev.off()
```

Run the script:

After this script executes, a file called *"rainfall_bar_chart.png"* will be created in the working directory and this is what it will look like:

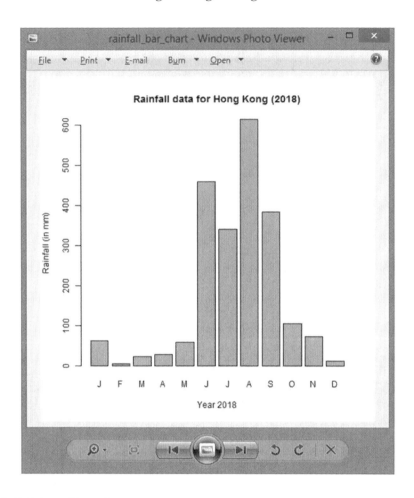

19.3 Line Graph

A line graph or a line chart is a statistical graphic similar to bar chart but instead of using bars to represent values, points are used and all the points are connected using straight lines. In R, there is a function called ***plot ()*** which is used to draw line graphs. General Syntax:

plot(<x>, <y>, <type>, <col>, <xlab>, <ylab>, <main>)
Where:
<x> - Values of x axis points

\<y\> - *Corresponding y value of each x value*

\<type\> - *Can be set to p, l or o — "p" draws only points, "l" draws only lines and "o" draws points and a line that connects these points.*

\<xlab\> - *Label for x-axis*

\<ylab\> - *Label for y-axis*

\<col\> - *Colour of the points/line.*

\<main\> - *Title of the line graph.*

When you call this function through the R terminal, a window will pop-up which will contain the line graph. If you want to write a script to plot a line graph, you will have to save it to a file. The procedure is similar to the one mentioned at the end of **Section 19.1** which explains how to create a pie chart using an R script; except, you need to call **plot( )** function instead of **pie( )** function in **Step 2**.

Here is monthly mean temperature data taken from the year 1981 to 2010 for the city of Taipei provided by the Central Weather Bureau of Taiwan.

Month	Mean Temperature (°C)
January	16.1
February	16.5
March	18.5
April	21.9
May	25.2
June	27.7
July	29.6
August	29.2
September	27.4
October	24.5
November	21.5
December	17.9

Let us create month and mean temperature vectors. In a line plot, x and y axis can be given a label but each point cannot be given an individual label and they take only numeric values. Hence, for month we will take values from 1 to 12.

month <- c(1:12)

temp <- c(16.1 ,16.5 ,18.5 ,21.9 ,25.2 ,27.7 ,29.6 ,29.2 ,27.4, 24.5 ,21.5, 17.9)

Call the plot function as follows:

plot (month, temp, type = "o", xlab = "Month", ylab = "Temperature in deg. Celcius", col = "blue", main = "Mean Temperature Data for Taipei (1981-2010)")

You should see a line graph like this:

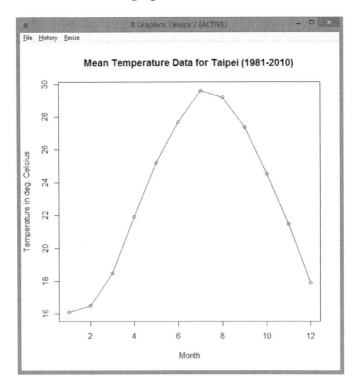

19. Data Visualization

Now, let us write an R script to generate the same line graph programmatically and save it as an image. We will name this file as **"temperature_line_graph.png"**, set *col* to *"red"* in the plot function.

```
#Line Graph Demo
#Set working directory
#IMPORTANT: SET YOUR OWN DIRECTORY WHICH IS ACCESSIBLE
setwd("F:/R")
#Create requisite vectors for plotting line chart
month <- c(1:12)
temp <- c(16.1 ,16.5 ,18.5 ,21.9 ,25.2 ,27.7 ,29.6 ,29.2 ,27.4, 24.5 ,21.5, 17.9)
#Set output image file name where the line graph will be saved
png ( file = "temperature_line_graph.png")
#Call the bar plot function
plot(month, temp, type = "o", xlab = "Month", ylab = "Temperature in deg. Celcius", col = "red", main = "Mean Temperature Data for Taipei (1981-2010)")
#Close the plotting device. I.e. Save the output file
dev.off()
```

Run the script:

Open the temperature_line_graph.png file from the working directory. It should look like this:

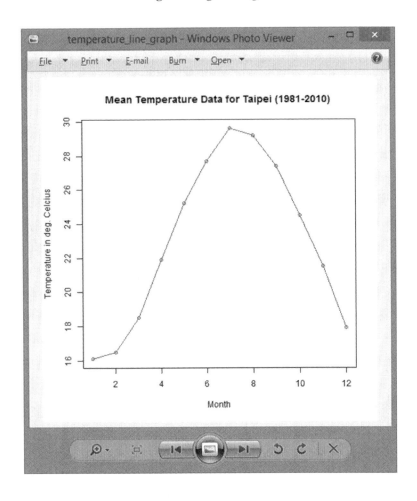

20. Programming Examples

20.1 Sum, Average and Greatest element of a vector.

Let us write an R script to find the sum, average and largest element of a vector without using built-in functions.

```r
#Sum Avg and Greatest element of a Vector
#Create a vector of arbitrary values
x <- c(3,8, 14.8, 9.46, 89, -6, 4.86, -23.4, 12, 65.75, -7.5)
#Find length
len <- length (x)
#Find sum of all elements
#initialize sum variable to 0
sum_x = 0
#Consider 1st element is the greatest
greatest = x[1]
for (val in x) {
   sum_x = (sum_x + val)
   #Check if the current element is greater than the greatest
   if (val > greatest) {
        #Assign val to greatest
        greatest = val
        }
    }
#Calculate average
avg_x = sum_x / len
#Display everything
cat("\nVector x:\n\n")
print (x)
cat("\n\nNumber of elements: ", len, "\nSum: ", sum_x, "Average: ", avg_x, "Greatest: ", greatest, "\n\n")
```

Output:

```
F:\R>Rscript sumavgmax.r
Vector x:
 [1]   3.00   8.00  14.80   9.46  89.00  -6.00   4.86 -23.40  12.00  65.75
[11]  -7.50

Number of elements:  11
Sum:   169.97 Average:   15.45182 Greatest:  89

F:\R>
```

20.2 Factorial

Factorial of a number *n* is given by *n!* where *n! = n x (n – 1) x (n – 2) x ... x 1*. For example, *5! = 5 x 4 x 3 x 2 x 1 = 120*. Factorial of a negative number cannot be calculated and *factorial of 0 is 1*. Let us write a function to calculate the factorial of a given number.

```
#Factorial of a number
#Function to find factorial
findFactorial <- function(n) {
   #Calculate Factorial
   f = 1
   while (n > 0) {
        f = f * n
        n = n - 1
        }
   return (f)
}
#Execution begins here
#Ask the user to enter an integer, read as integer
cat("\n Enter a number: ")
input_num <- readLines("stdin", n = 1)
num = as.numeric(input_num)
#Call factorial, pass num as argument
f = findFactorial(num)
#Display
cat("\nFactorial of", num, "is: ", f, "\n\n")
```

Output:

```
F:\R>Rscript factorial.r
 Enter a number: 0
Factorial of 0 is:  1

F:\R>Rscript factorial.r
 Enter a number: 6
Factorial of 6 is:  720

F:\R>
```

20.3 Reverse a given number

Let us write an R script to reverse a given number.

```
#Reverse a given number
#Ask the user to enter an integer, read as integer
cat("\n Enter a number: ")
input_num <- readLines("stdin", n = 1)
reverse = 0 ;
num = as.numeric(input_num)
#Loop while number is non-zero
while ( num ) {
   #Multiply 10 to rev to shift it by one place
   #Add one's digit to rev
   reverse = (reverse * 10 ) + ( num %% 10 ) ;
   #Discard one's digit using integer by integer
   division
   num = num %/% 10 ;
   }
cat("\n\nReverse:", reverse, "\n\n")
```

Output:

```
F:\R>Rscript reverse.r
 Enter a number: 45723

Reverse: 32754

F:\R>
```

20.4 CSV to XLSX File conversion

In this example, we will learn how can we programmatically convert a CSV file to an Excel Spreadsheet (XLSX file). The idea is simple – open the CSV file, read the data into a data frame, write the same data frame to an output XLSX file. Two important things to note here – working directory should be set to the one where the source CSV file is present and "xlsx" package should be loaded at the beginning of the script. We will use the *student_data.csv* file from *Section 18.1* which looks like this:

```
id,name,stream,country,marks
1,Alexa,IT,Cyprus,65.8
2,Harvey,Electrical,UK,93.6
3,Gabriela,Telecommunication,Brazil,78.4
4,Ying,IT,China,81.5
5,Steven,Mechanical,UK,97.3
6,Jessica,IT,USA,68.4
7,Lee,Electrical,China,59.4
```

Here is the R script:

```
#CSV to XSLX Conversion
#Load xlsx package
library("xlsx")
#Set Working Directory
setwd("F:/R/")
#Read CSV file, store in a data frame
student_df        <-        read.csv("student_data.csv",
stringsAsFactors = FALSE)
#Display Data Frame
cat("\nOriginal CSV File:\n")
print (student_df)
#Write the data frame student_dfto Excel Spreadsheet
write.xlsx(student_df                                    ,
"student_data_converted.xlsx", row.names = FALSE )
cat("\nData        Frame        written        to
student_data_converted.xlsx \n\n")
```

20. Programming Examples

Run this script:

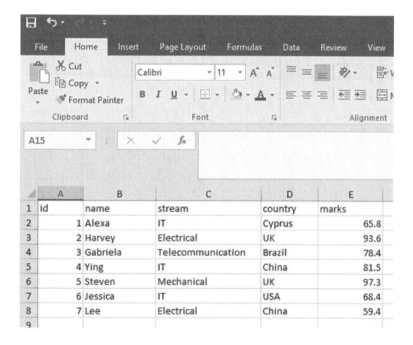

Here is what the converted Excel sheet looks like:

	A	B	C	D	E
1	id	name	stream	country	marks
2	1	Alexa	IT	Cyprus	65.8
3	2	Harvey	Electrical	UK	93.6
4	3	Gabriela	Telecommunication	Brazil	78.4
5	4	Ying	IT	China	81.5
6	5	Steven	Mechanical	UK	97.3
7	6	Jessica	IT	USA	68.4
8	7	Lee	Electrical	China	59.4

20.5 Sine Wave Generation

Sine is a trigonometric function of an angle. In a right angle triangle, Sine of an angle is the ratio of the length of the opposite side (opposite to the angle in question) to the length of the hypotenuse. R has an inbuilt function called *sin(<angle>)* which returns the *Sine* of the given *<angle>*. The *<angle>* should be specified in **radians** and not in **degrees**. Mathematically speaking, the Sine function has a period of 2π. That is, after this interval, the values are going to repeat. To plot *Sine* wave, we will use *seq* function to generate values of an angle from $-\pi$ to $+\pi$ with a step of 0.1 and store them in a vector called *x*. Closer the values, smoother will be the wave. We will create another vector to store Sine values of *x*. Using *plot( )* function, we will plot the points of *x* vs *Sine(x)* and store it in a file called *sine_wave.png*. The option *type* will be set to *"l"* as we only want to see a smooth Sine curve, not really the data points. We have studied in *Section 19.3* that *plot* function is used to draw line graph. If the points are close enough, the combination of lines connecting the points is going to look like a curve.

```
#Sine Wave Generation
#Set working directory
#IMPORTANT: SET YOUR OWN DIRECTORY WHICH IS ACCESSIBLE
setwd("F:/R")
#Create requisite vectors for plotting line graph
x <- seq(-pi, pi, 0.1)
sine_x <- sin(x)
#Set output image file name where the sine wave will be saved
png ( file = "sine_wave.png")
#Call the bar plot function
plot(x, sine_x, type = "l", xlab = "x", ylab = "Sine(x)", col = "blue", main = "Sine Wave from -pi to +pi")
```

Run the script:

```
F:\R>Rscript sinewave.r
F:\R>
```

Output Image File (sine_wave.png):

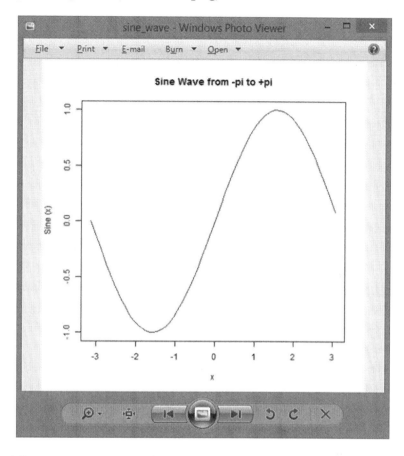

There are many more built-in mathematical functions in R such as *cos, tan, log, etc*. You can try to plot their curves.

21. Final Words

In this book, I have covered the basics of R programming which is enough to familiarize with this language. R provides very powerful tools for data analysis, data visualization, statistical computing, etc. If you are interested in any of these topics, there are plenty of resources online which can help you learn more. This is an age of data. Huge chunks of data are generated by applications, devices, networks, etc. There is a need of analysing this data which can aid in better decision making as well as in process improvement.

Hope you have learned something valuable from this book. I wish you all the best!

If you enjoyed this book as much as I've enjoyed writing it, you can subscribe* to my email list for exclusive content and sneak peaks of my future books.

Visit the link below:

http://eepurl.com/du_L4n

OR

Use the QR Code:

(*Must be 13 years or older to subscribe)

Made in the USA
Columbia, SC
03 December 2022